# GEORGE TOOKER
## WORKING DRAWINGS

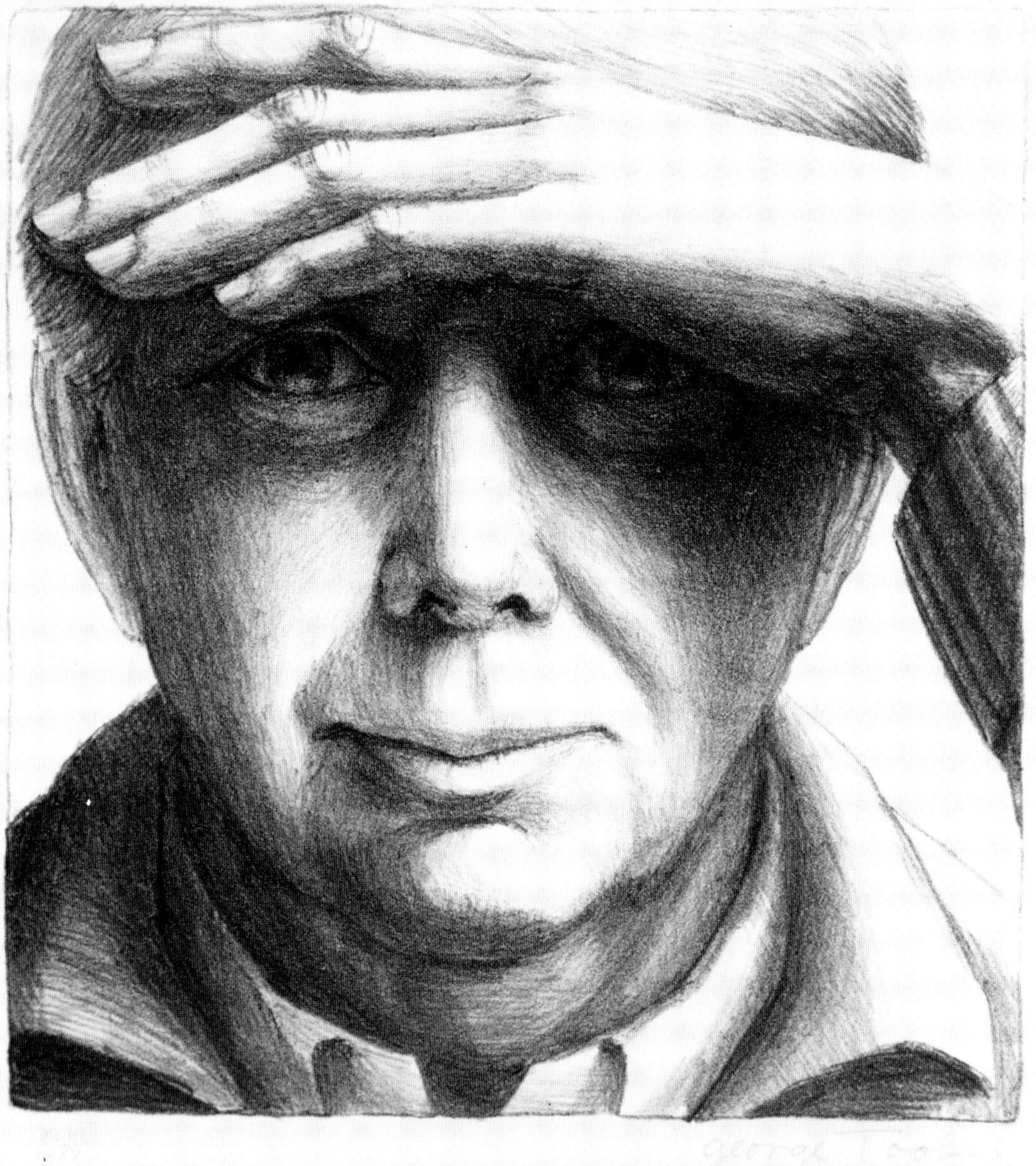

2

# GEORGE TOOKER
## WORKING DRAWINGS

Ildiko Heffernan

An exhibition organized by
Robert Hull Fleming Museum
University of Vermont
Burlington, Vermont

This catalog was published for the exhibition:

GEORGE TOOKER: WORKING DRAWINGS
Robert Hull Fleming Museum
University of Vermont, Burlington, Vermont
11 September–1 November, 1987



ISBN #0-934658-03-X

Cover illustrations: Studies for *Window I*, 1955

Frontispiece: *Self-Portrait*, lithograph, 1984

Catalog design by Mary Ann Ricketson
Printed in the U.S. by Villanti & Sons Printers, Inc., Williston, Vermont

This catalog and exhibition have been made possible with funds from the Friends of the Fleming.

# CONTENTS

PAGES

# ACKNOWLEDGMENTS

I am personally gratified that George Tooker accorded the Robert Hull Fleming Museum of the University of Vermont the privilege of exhibiting his working drawings. I wish to express our deepest appreciation to the time and effort he has put into helping us. I am especially grateful for his generosity not only in letting us show these personal works, but also for speaking so frankly about himself and his working process to me. Without his considerable help, my essay could not have been written.

Since 1980 I have wanted to have an exhibition of George Tooker's works at the Museum. It has taken these years for us to be able to do so. In some ways it has worked for the better as originally we were to show his paintings only and now we are able to show his drawings which have never been seen by the public. We look upon the occasion of his exhibition as an important event for the Museum in featuring the work of one of the important American painters of this century who has been a resident of Vermont for the past twenty-five years.

As with any project of this scope, it takes the efforts of many individuals to make it a success. Our sincere thanks are extended to the lenders of the paintings in the exhibition: Walker Art Center, Mr. and Mrs. Joel Harnett, Kitty and Herbert Glantz, Frank Mainzer, Steven and Channa Wintner, the Addison Gallery of American Art at Phillips Academy, George Tooker, and three private collectors who wish to remain anonymous.

Additionally, our appreciation is extended to Thomas Garver and Arnold Skolnick, as well as Glenn McMillen of the Marisa del Re Gallery, for providing assistance with the organization of the exhibition. My thanks are extended to Henry Ratner, who helped with the copy and editing of the manuscript, and to Champlain Color Corporation for donating several color separations.

My special thanks are extended to the wonderful people on the Museum staff: Ann Porter, Acting Curator, who accompanied me to George Tooker's studio and helped conceptualize the exhibition and select the works; David Penney, our Registrar, whose patient arrangements made it easier for all of us; Merlin Acomb, Exhibition Designer/Preparator, whose highly professional installation makes the exhibition a success; Mary Ann Ricketson, whose creative efforts are evident in the catalog design; Anna Seyller, whose patient, painstaking editing helped me immeasurably to write my essay, and to Pat Brennan, the Museum's Secretary, for her unfailing attention to detail.

Ildiko Heffernan

# THE WORKING DRAWINGS OF GEORGE TOOKER

George Tooker is best known for the gem-like egg tempera paintings with which he first came to the American public's attention in the late 1940's in major exhibitions of American painters at the Museum of Modern Art and the Whitney Museum of American Art in New York City. His oeuvre consists primarily of representational paintings with "content" in a century when non-objective abstraction has been the stylistic preference of the artistic mainstream. Throughout his career, Tooker has steadily painted in the painstaking Renaissance medium of egg tempera on gesso panel completing only two, three, maybe up to five paintings a year. In the past decade he has tried his hand at printmaking, with seven lithographs and two intaglios reiterating themes of his paintings. For all of these finished works he has produced preliminary and working drawings.

Tooker's preoccupation with his painting and the use of drawings to provide the mode for developing them is directly attributable to his early training at the Art Students League in New York City. He readily recognizes the considerable impact that his relatively short time at the League, from 1943–1945, had upon him. He not only found the means of working and the philosophical basis for his future work but also formed lifelong friendships. "I was absolutely delighted to go to an art school and I had some wonderful teachers. Reginald Marsh was a marvelous teacher, a wonderful artist and man. Kenneth Hayes Miller was very ill by the time I was there in 1943, but I remember him as a great lecturer, a spellbinding speaker, very inspirational. Paul Cadmus became my closest friend and started me painting in egg tempera on panel. I must also say Harry Sternberg was awfully good to me." (1) Their early influence has permeated Tooker's work and life. All of the teachers at the League were concerned with the 1930's American revival of Renaissance techniques of draughtsmanship, composition and execution. These ideas and concepts influenced him a great deal, as you can see from his work over the years. However, what is most impressive is not how well Tooker assimilated these influences, but how successfully he created his own distinctive style and singular voice in addressing the issues and concerns important to him.

Tooker frequently acknowledges other artists past and present as sources of inspiration for his own works. When asked who he has looked to specifically for his own work, Tooker responds, "I don't know where to start." He points out that, "I have very eclectic tastes and love the work of so many artists, Europeans and Americans. Of course, I have always loved the early Italians—Giotto, Fra Angelico, Piero della Francesca, Masaccio, Botticelli, Mantegna, Simone Martini, among others. I love the early Sienese painters for their wonderful use of color and the Florentines for their composition and volumetric forms." Motifs, forms, and compositional elements have appeared and continue to appear throughout Tooker's works from these artists. Tooker adds, "the seventeenth-century Spanish painters—Velasquez, Ribera—and the early Romanesque Catalonian Chapel fresco painters are also favorites of mine. Others are the French—Ingres, for his forms, and Georges de la Tours for his use of light; and the early nineteenth-century Americans—Bingham and Mount". As for his twentieth-century influences and favorites, in addition to those already mentioned, Hopper is a strong influence. As so many other artists in the twentieth-century, Tooker acknowledges that he has also been influenced by Picasso, but only by his early classical period. He concludes that the reason he looks a great deal at paintings by other artists is that he sees them all as "my teachers and as source of inspiration for my own work."



by
Ildiko
Heffernan

In this tradition going back to the Renaissance masters, Tooker has produced a considerable body of drawings done in preparation for his paintings and prints. The egg tempera process requires an exactitude of execution with no room for changes during the process of painting. It necessitates a carefully conceived design and composition to be worked out prior to beginning the painting. Numerous preliminary drawings and a final drawing used as a cartoon to transfer the image to the gessoed panel need to be developed as part of such a process. Tooker has at least one cartoon drawing and often several preliminary drawings for each work. These drawings are the sole record of his widely dispersed paintings in public and private collections. When queried about his working method, Tooker says, "It is probably just my temperament. I really am more comfortable working in this way. It is a mode that has served me well."

Since his student days Tooker has not engaged in drawing for its own sake. He kept sketchbooks then "to train my hand and eye. I was drawing all of the time, learning to draw people. While I was at Harvard, and even before then when I was a teenager, I would draw a lot of watercolor landscapes for pocket money which the Women's Exchange would sell for me." With the exception of these student works, his drawings have not been made for public viewing, but are "a tool, a guide for me to use to work out my ideas and feelings. I liken the function of my final preliminary drawing to that served by the architect's blueprint for his building. All of them are truly 'messy working drawings' in every sense of the word."

His approach to drawing differs both stylistically and technically from his paintings. While his paintings rely principally on various degrees of shading through the use of color, his drawings are almost purely linear with only occasional shading and detailed rendering of forms. Interestingly, he draws the way that he paints—one brush stroke at a time. In his paintings the strokes blend together, but in his drawings each pencil line remains visible, even in the shaded areas, creating an entirely different impact. "I see my paintings as closer to abstractions, composed of the juxtaposition of colors and forms to evoke a feeling, while my drawings remain primarily linear." Most of the time his drawings are on tracing paper. He generally makes a single image or composition on each sheet. He writes notes on the edge of the page: colors he plans to use and their emotive analogue, notations about various measurements, the mood or idea he wishes to convey, or the title for the work. Occasionally he makes sketches of a new figure or composition on a sheet used for studies for another work. A small cursory compositional sketch for *Entertainers*(1959–1960) is included on one of the detail face studies for *Sleepers II*(1957), basically remaining the same in the finished work completed two years later. In some initial sketches he uses the same sheet to experiment with variations of an idea, as he does in those for *Sleepers I*(1951) and *II*(1957), *Embrace I*(1979) and *Meadow II*(1977–79), but it is not his usual working method.

Most frequently his drawings are pencil sketches delineating only the essential forms of the overall composition. These compositional drawings are quite intricate and carefully developed as the underlying structure and perspective of the painting is visibly plotted. He often draws the outline of the horizontal or vertical rectangle or the square shape of the painting as a border before sketching the figure(s) or working on the compositional elements. He then plots out a web of diagonals to define the perspective with vanishing points beyond the picture plane providing a strong angling and diagonal thrust. He frequently uses a triangular compositional format, often with multiple overlapping triangles. Sometimes a series of them recede into the distance while other times they are only partially contained within the picture plane. Tooker is not happy with the linear quality his drawings assume, even though this is almost predetermined by the nature of the technical problems they are meant to resolve.

Valuing versatility, Tooker prefers to use tracing paper for most of his drawings. This makes it possible to simultaneously retain the original concept and to look at the image in different ways. Tooker especially appreciates the paper's transparency, a quality which enables him to see the image from a new perspective each time. Using transparent paper makes it unnecessary to erase and he is assured that nothing is lost while exploring ideas, colors or changing the composition. This way, each drawing is a starting point for exploring the next facet or problem at the same time as it remains an unchanged visual record of the experiments undertaken. A most interesting use of this device is in two small color sketches for *Window I* (1955). On a single strip of tracing paper, within two thick-lined borders, the same image is drawn upside-down. When the paper is folded in half they merge as one, with the colors and lines visible from one to the other, making it possible to judge what does and does not work in the composition. He usually makes drawings on separate pieces of paper, however, and then juxtaposes them as he continues to make variations or changes in the composition.

*fig. 2 (cover)*

Even though it is the construction of the painting that is of primary concern to him, the composition has to develop organically into a final design that is an outgrowth of the subject and content of the painting. What Jared French once said to him has remained a guiding principle: "The design of a picture is very important and there is no way to make a well-designed painting unless it comes out of its meaning." Tooker works very hard to resolve these issues before he begins to paint and his working drawings are visual testimony to this process. Because of this, the changes are more numerous and are executed in greater detail for those images in which he is concerned with developing a new content. The numerous drawings for the first two *Sleepers* and the *Lovers* series are a good example of this process.

*fig. 17–20*

Although remaining a figurative painter, Tooker has not felt the need to use live models since his early years, being interested only in making his figures believable in terms of his concerns. "Like Ingres, I wish to convey the emotive quality, to show the feeling." He uses anatomical distortion to get an idea or feeling across. He did have his friends pose for his early works, especially when working on *Coney Island* (1948), *Children and Spastics* (1946) and *The Market* (1949). He continues to use his own figure, face or hands as models for his drawing studies as well as for several self-portraits.

After transferring the major shapes and forms from the drawing onto the gessoed panel, he makes no other major changes. Some minor adjustments may be required to angle the composition differently or make it more faceted. Otherwise he does not wish to be conscious of the drawing throughout the process of painting. Even though a great deal of technical control and intellectual speculation are evident throughout his working process, it is intuitively that he determines when the design and composition work. Both the design and the composition have to be exact for Tooker. He takes all the time necessary until he is satisfied before he begins to paint. On the other hand, it is also important to him that the drawing remain 'unfinished'. "I want to resolve only the principal forms and shapes to leave room for the painting to develop slowly during the process of painting. For me the painting needs to evolve, to be created. It takes me a long time to formulate the idea and clearly define the concept. I use drawing as a means of doing so, making a series of them to explore an idea until it strikes me as right. I don't like to explain what I am doing in words. If I did I would explain it away and lose it. I need to keep the energy in, reserve it, to use in the actual performance of the painting."

When Tooker is working on a painting he does not spend time drawing. However, between paintings, "I always continue to work on a regular basis at my drawing board in my studio, exploring ideas by sketching, maybe only doodling with a pencil, waiting to have something strike a spark. If I didn't do this, I could lose an idea I want to use. During these times I may go back to my earlier drawings to try to capture a spark there that I want to get back to, or when I am stuck, I try to use them to inspire a new work. It doesn't always work though, and I just have to continue to work at it until something feels right."

This is usually a very stressful period for him. The time can seem very long between the two, maybe five, paintings he works on each year, even though it takes months to finish each. Tooker observes that frequently he does not know what the next painting will be and always worries that another painting won't happen. "It is very difficult for me not to have a painting in the works. There is a certain amount of panic each time."

He keeps all of his drawings and refers back to them for inspiration, or to work out a composition, design or detail in a new work. When he has problems with a painting, or at the outset of a new theme, he will use drawings more than usual. *fig. 8–12* *Subway* (1950) posed a challenge with its complex multiple perspective. The faces and figures of the man and woman in the foreground were difficult to resolve. Tooker made a number of preliminary sketches working out the perspective grid, the outline of forms and the placement of the figures. Finely executed, delicately shaded detailed drawings of the man's and woman's face were made at this planning stage and appear relatively unchanged in the painting. The *Sleepers II* (1957) composition and the exact rendering of the faces gave him a great deal of problems, and numerous drawings in various stages of completion exist for it. However, not every painting requires such painstaking attention. Some work out easily and are quickly resolved. Only one cursory sketch with a few lines barely outlining the principal shapes and forms exists for the painting *The Waiting Room* (1959), besides the final cartoon drawing. For *Bathers* (1950), only one final drawing was necessary. This pattern has not changed over the years. Some paintings continue to give him trouble, requiring numerous sketches and/or detailed drawings, while for others everything works right away. For his most recent work, *Window 1987* (1987), he made four drawings, while for *Corporate Decision* (1983), almost a dozen sketches were necessary to resolve the background figural group abstracted from a corporate annual report.

Tooker uses some of his drawings, especially figural forms, groupings and facial types, as prototypes to be used later as patterns to incorporate into newer works. The drawings for *Mirror I* (1962) are a good example of this, as Tooker needs to create forms and a composition to convey the completely new emotive content he wishes to achieve. He draws numerous small compositional sketches to satisfactorily place the principal oval shapes of the mirror and the woman's head with the partial skull in the background. He draws several large ones, experimenting with the shading and expression of the face, the placement of the hands, and the fall and patterning of the drapery. The perfect ovoid of the face which he finally settles upon for the painting vaguely echoes those in *Sleepers*. He does create a completely new composition and figural forms for what is to become the first of a series of four Mirror paintings and the source for a number of other paintings. *Toilette* (1962), *Table I* (1959) and *Table II* (1981) also use the facial type and the 'Vanitas' motif developed for *Mirror I*. The following year, for *Mirror II* (1963), he changes the composition and again makes numerous drawings and sketches. In this composition he replaces the oval mirror with a rectangular one, the skull with the face of an old woman, while the two faces look open-eyed into the mirror partially obstructing the young woman's face. *Mirror IV* (1976–79), painted more than a decade later, draws upon both previous paintings, eliminates the second face from the first *Mirror* and uses the composition from the second one. For this he does not feel the need to make many additional drawings; a few preliminary drawings and a final cartoon suffice.

The original drawings for the surreal images of the "floating" faces in *Sleepers II* (1957) serve as *fig. 17–20* the source several years later for the face of the woman in *Meadow I* (1960–61) and again in the other commemorative painting, *Meadow II* (1977–79). This 1970's painting echoes the composition of the first Meadow and again uses the face first developed for the 1957 *Sleepers*. The principal components of the design—the two-figure composition, the woman lying with eyes closed on the ground next to a kneeling man with downcast eyes within a grassy meadow and a stand of trees in the background—were resolved in the first *Meadow*. However, Tooker feels a need to change from a horizontal orientation to a vertical one, placing increased emphasis upon the man, his face and hands now subsumed with sadness, and only the face of the other figure included. He makes numerous drawings and sketches to get the kneeling figure of the man just right with the placement of his hands on both knees carefully conceived, his face now more clearly a self-portrait and a deep-felt expression of watchful mourning permeating the entire composition.

A few of his drawings incorporate color. Several drawings are carefully worked while others are rough, tiny color compositions. For *Toilette* (1962), two delicate color washes on tracing paper exist *fig. 21, 22, 24, 26* while in two others, white wash is used sparingly to give the barest indication of shading. *Window II* (1956) has several small pastel drawings on tracing paper, a large finished drawing with some white and color wash, and a tiny watercolor sketch that is closest to the painting. For a full-size study of *Mirror II* (1963) on transparent drafting paper he uses color wash. Color drawings for his first *Self-Portrait* (1947), *Lovers I* (1959), *Lovers II* (1962), *Gypsy* (1951), *Gypsies* (1968), *Meadow I* (1960–61) and *Embrace I* (1979) use gouache, watercolor, crayon, colored pencil, tempera or color wash throughout. Drawings for *Festa* (1948), *Sleepers II* (1957), *Government Bureau* (1956), *Mirror I* (1962), *Odalisque* (1967), and *Window 1987* (1987) use white wash or white conté crayon sparingly for highlighting only, and sometimes in combination with another color or two.

Tooker uses detailed finished drawings as an implement to trace directly onto the actual surface of a painting. He had so much trouble getting the face of the man right in *Festa* (1948) that he traces his drawing directly to the prepared painting surface. Other times, it is at the painting stage that the final shape of the figural or facial characteristics are worked out. The woman's face in *Window II* (1956) and the man's profile in *Lovers I* (1959) change considerably from the detailed finished draw- *fig. 27* ings to the painting. He is not satisfied with the man's face in this *Lovers* until he resolves it during the process of painting. He includes a woman's face in his preliminary drawings and sketches for this painting, but settles for showing only her hair, as he is most concerned with conveying the sweeping gesture of an all-engulfing, universal love with both figures seen as a single form occupying the same space.

Tooker's paintings each explore one of several parallel "themes" which consistently concern him and which he develops in several 'series' of paintings. These 'series' are not necessarily initially conceived as such by Tooker; rather, he picks up 'threads' of concerns over the years and elaborates upon them, at times, years later. Much of his work can be placed into identifiable series, a categorization which is most completely presented in Thomas Garver's 1985 *George Tooker* monograph. Tooker's works could be broadly conceived to fall into five principal series of works by the themes they explore: 1) the early work covering a range of themes and subject matter mostly in urban settings; 2) the "public" paintings of social concern; 3) contemplative paintings of man perceiving his own essence within a timeless and boundless universe; 4) paintings of man's relationships with himself and others; and 5) metaphysical paintings of human love as a transcendent manifestation of a mystical, eternal love permeating reality. The roots of these themes go back to his early paintings, with the exception of this latest, 'metaphysical' series, which he began after his conversion to Catholicism in the 1970's.

Preliminary and final cartoon drawings from his major series are included in this exhibition with a number of their related paintings. He pursues a wider range of themes in his early works than he pursues later. Some of these he returns to, others he abandons. Among these early works are urban street, beach and amusement park scenes and a miscellany of other figural compositions on a variety of themes. Representing this early period in this exhibition are a preliminary and a final drawing for *Festa* (1948) and a final drawing for *Bathers* (1950). Festa depicts a street festival scene in New York City's Little Italy, close in figural composition and style to the work of Reginald Marsh, with whom he was studying and friends with at the time. However, the volumetric solidity of the Renaissance-like architectural elements and strong diagonal orientation of the perspective recall de Chirico's surreal environments in composition and feeling. Although he shortly abandons Marsh's 'baroque' figural style, he does retain the juxtaposition of ambiguous, almost contradictory elements to convey a feeling of discomfort, of figures isolated within an environment radically different from their own essence.

The ready availability of Tooker's own image prompts him to use it repeatedly when in need of a model. It is a practice he begins early in his career and continues to this day. Tooker first includes his own figure in the 1945 painting he now regards as his first mature work. In *Audience* (1945) (not included in this exhibition), the semi-nude male figure is identifiably the artist with brush in hand, working on a drawing. The preparatory and final studies for *Meadow II* (1977–79), in which the mourner watching over the dead figure next to him is in fact Tooker, are included in this exhibition.

In addition to using his own image in many of his paintings, Tooker has produced four self-portraits: two paintings more than twenty years apart, the first in 1947 and the second in 1969; and most recently two lithographs in 1984 and 1985. Represented in this exhibition are preliminary and final drawings for the two paintings and the 1984 lithograph. The most elaborate and detailed preliminary drawings are for the 1947 *Self-Portrait*, inspired by a desire to create an image for a circular frame. This is his only painting with a tondo format. The three drawings for this enigmatic self-portrait are the earliest in this show. Interestingly, the lovely, full-color gouache drawing for this self-portrait is quite detailed and close to being finished, but differs substantially from the finished painting. He works at placing on a circular plane a rigidly frontal image in a classical triangular composition. He makes numerous notations on his drawing about his planned use of color, assigning emotive qualities to them, only to change the colors completely in the painting. One of these notes on the drawing states his aim to illuminate the composition with a "cold light from above." This creates a 'surreal' mood in the painting. It is in the small cursory sketches that the final composition and shading are worked out. The later self-portraits require far less effort as they use the more traditional rectangular or square picture plane. Included in this exhibition is the final drawing for the 1969 *Self-Portrait*, a straightforward black and white pencil sketch of the artist with brush in hand. The composition remains basically unchanged in the painting.

*fig. 7*



Tooker develops a number of paintings using distinctively early Renaissance figures and compositions. He depicts a universal mankind suspended in time within a clearly delineated space imbued with a spiritual, metaphysical import going beyond the immediacy of the scene. Of these, *Bathers* (1948) is represented in this exhibition. The drawing works out a complex perspective to achieve a finely balanced composition suffused with light. This beautifully simple, classical composition is distinctively Tooker's style.

The best known of his painting series are the so-called "public paintings" of social commentary and are represented in this exhibition by drawings for *Subway* (1950), *Government Bureau* (1956), *The Waiting Room* (1959), and *Corporate Decision* (1983). There are fewer preliminary drawings for this group as a whole than would be expected given the importance and prominence they hold in his work. There are four small preparatory sketches and one full-size final cartoon drawing for *Subway*; two small sketches for *Government Bureau*, in addition to the full size drawing; as mentioned for *The Waiting Room* only a small sketch and the final drawing are made; while *Corporate Decision* did require more sketches than the others. *fig. 8–12*

The earlier works have in common a precise geometric composition: oblique angling, complex sources of light and the strongly receding diagonals of multiple perspectives, creating an uneasy ordering of the environment in which ambiguous figures are placed. The often faceless, stolid figures are defined as heavy, volumetric forms. Each is isolated from the other, locked in its own body and immobilized within a confined space, as it is pushed and pulled by the conflicting forces of its environment. The preliminary sketches for *Subway* show Tooker's concern with defining the strong diagonal, inward thrust of the perspective to create a force pulling us into a rapidly receding space. He works at delineating the principal spatial partitions and the placement of the figures. On one of the sheets he carefully finishes a small drawing of the woman's head in the foreground with the agonized expression exactly as it appears in the painting. On the same sheet there is another finished drawing, this one of the man in profile standing in the first cubicle behind and to the side of the woman. A tiny sketch of the composition is also on this page as well as an outline sketch of another male figure which does not appear in the painting. Another page again has the detailed drawing of the man in partial profile and the full face of the woman, but includes three other figures. One of them is the torso of the man appearing directly behind the woman in the painting; the second is the half-length figure of the man in the first booth, and the third, the back of a man's head, which is not used. Tooker has written on the drawing "Telefonate alla questura." The large finished drawing for the painting is fascinating for the spiderweb-like diagonal lines which are the visible underpinning of the composition. In the borders of this sheet Tooker has printed his name several times, repeatedly writing some of the letters, seemingly practicing the form his signature should take. Some other sketches, apparently doodlings, are also in these margins. Three other compositional sketches exist, two on the same sheet, another more detailed one on a separate page. This later one has several notations on the bottom: "do with closer vanishing points," "change proportions to 2 to 3 also," and "move central up to light." Even though the finished painting is very close to the drawing, some differences remain, especially in the development of the right-hand side of the composition, where several figures have been added during the painting process. *fig. 8–12* *fig. 9* *fig. 10* *fig. 8*

Despite the significance of these "public" paintings, the greater portion of Tooker's oeuvre is very intimate and personal. These works can be seen as three distinct groups. Those that look at man in a contemplative state of "being" beyond space and time are most clearly presented in Tooker's *Sleepers* series of four paintings and a number of other related works. These are peopled by beings suspended in a timeless, ambiguous space. Representing *Sleepers* in this exhibition are four small preliminary sketches for *Sleepers I* (1951); one preliminary and a final cartoon drawing for *Sleepers IV* (1978); four large drawings for *Sleepers II* (1957); several smaller studies of the head, one on which a small sketch of the thematically related *Entertainers* (1959–60) is also included; and one which has three very cursive compositional sketches. One of the large drawings has very carefully delineated *fig. 13–20*

faces, with especially delicately rendered areas around the eyes. That he works hard to get the faces exactly right and experiments extensively with the composition to serve his conception is especially evident in these often painstakingly executed preliminary drawings. Two very rough pencil sketches
*fig. 13* for *Sleepers I* on blue notepaper and two others on a single sheet torn from a larger sheet of drawing paper indicate the basics of the final composition actually used in the painting. There are prelimi-
*fig. 15, 16* nary and final cartoon drawings on tracing paper for *Sleepers IV* which are directly derived from the earlier *Sleepers I*. The composition and figures of the earlier work are used as prototypes, but are simplified. One of the three original supine figures is eliminated and the craggy landscape is reduced to undulating lines indicative of the patterning of the sand upon which the figures lie. The paintings remain close in conception to these sets of drawings and no major changes are made during the process of painting.

Related to these are his two memorial paintings, *Meadow I* (1960–61), painted upon his mother's death, and *Meadow II* (1977–79), after his close friend and companion William Christopher died. The painting *Meadow I* with the nine accompanying studies for it and four drawings for Meadow II are included in this exhibition. Additionally, he develops this meditative theme of a watchful figure in other paintings. A final drawing for *Night I* (1963) and the *Odalisque* (1967) painting with its two full-size studies examine his further development of this theme as a part of this exhibition.

Another group of paintings looks at the essence of man's relationship with himself and his
*fig. 1–6 (cover)* "soul," his relationships with others, and his place in a timeless, boundless universe. *Window I* (1955), *Window IX* (1968), and his most recent painting, *Window 1987* (1987), are among these, as are *Gypsies* (1968) and *Toilette* (1962). Included in this exhibition are his first and most recent *Window* paintings with their related preliminary and final drawings. Seven drawings for *Gypsies* together with the painting look at this elaboration of the theme of man's relationships. *Toilette* is represented by two
*fig. 21–26* color drawings on tracing paper, a large graphite and white wash drawing on buff paper, two pencil sketches on tracing paper and a small sketch on a torn piece of drawing paper.

A further elaboration of this theme are the 'Vanitas'-type compositions reflecting upon the transitoriness of life. This concern is evident in the related series of *Mirror I* (1962) through *Mirror IV* (1976–79). Of these, five drawings selected from numerous drawings for *Mirror I* (1962) and one study and the painting of *Mirror II* (1964) are featured in this exhibition. The studies vary from very sketchy outlines of forms to several finely delineated, delicately shaded works. Both of these paintings are worked out in the drawing stage and remain relatively unchanged from the final sketch.

The most recent series has as its theme the 'miracle' of human love transformed into a metaphysical state of being with eternal validity. This theme evolves from *Lovers I* (1959) and *Lovers II*
*fig. 27–32* (1960) into his recent *Embrace* series: *Embrace I* (1979) through *Embrace VI* (1986); and the two *Embrace* lithographs, *Embrace I (Lovers)* (1982) and *Embrace II* (1984). Closely related to these is his *Embrace of Peace* (1986), with only one final cartoon study needed. In this exhibition some drawings from each of these paintings are included, as are the *Embrace II* (1981) and *Embrace IV* (1984) paintings, although a number of additional drawings exist.



The concept is first worked out in the drawings for *Lovers I* twenty years before he returns to recapture this feeling, recreating it as the first of his *Embrace* paintings. One final cartoon drawing, two pencil sketches and a small full-color watercolor study exist for this first *Lovers*, while for *Lovers II*, six pencil sketches and a final drawing are included in the exhibition. *Lovers I* focuses upon the man's embrace and the woman is indicated only by her embracing arm, her hair encircling the man's face in profile, and her body joining his as they both occupy the same space. In *Lovers II* he shifts the emphasis to the woman's embrace, showing both faces in profile, closer to being a depiction of a kiss reminiscent of Giotto's Visitation. The sweeping movement of *Lovers I* is recreated in the first two *Embrace* paintings while the others become more focused upon the encircling arms of the embracing couple, again in profile, retaining the feeling of a ritual symbolic expression of love between a man and a woman but evocative of a spiritual, almost mystical aura as first developed for the second *Lovers*. There are three studies for *Embrace I*, two on one small sheet of tracing paper, one of them in color. Additionally, he makes a detailed drawing of the woman's hand resting on the man's back. The cartoon drawing for *Embrace I* remains relatively unchanged in the painting. They show how Tooker has modified the sweeping horizontal movement of the figures from *Lovers* to a vertical composition. He is focusing upon the 'beatific' face of the woman, whose arms envelop the man in a tenderly loving embrace. Their figures appear to be encircled by the softly swaying ferns in the foreground as the gently undulating hills behind them serve as the setting for their love. For *Embrace II*, Tooker returns to the horizontal format and retains the figural composition and feeling used in the first *Embrace*, but places the figures within a more distant landscape of the same undulating hill with a sun half-visible in the distant horizon placed at the top of the composition. His *Embrace I (Lovers)* (1982) black and white lithograph uses this second *Embrace* painting's composition. The final drawing for the third *Embrace* (1983) is used for the painting. Tooker keeps the figural composition from the first *Lovers* but raises the figures to the upper half of the picture plane, placing greater emphasis upon the encircling arms and reinforcing them by the sweeping movement of the abstracted hills which seemingly engulf and protect the two figures in the foreground. The fourth *Embrace* in the final drawing relates most closely to *Embrace II* but the figures are higher in the picture plane, with the top of their heads crowding the upper edge of the composition. This places a greater emphasis upon the arms in the act of embracing, and the face of the woman is again close to Giotto's Virgin Mary in the Visitation. The *Embrace II* black and white lithograph is the same image as the *Embrace IV* painting.

*fig. 28, 29, 30*

*fig. 31*

*fig. 32*

The emotive quality of these two series is close to his more overtly "religious" paintings represented in this exhibition by three drawings for *Orant* (1977), painted in Spain shortly after his conversion to Catholicism. The drawings show a male figure with his two hands outstretched in supplication and his lips partially opened, actively calling forth in prayer. The drawings carefully work out the composition and the expressive content for the painting. The painting is basically the same as the preliminary drawings. One of these drawings is the final cartoon and has dry, red ochre pigment on its verso which Tooker used to transfer the drawing to the prepared surface of the painting.

All of the prints, with the exception of the *Self-Portraits*, reiterate themes from his paintings. The *Embrace I (Lovers I)* 1982 lithograph is the only one which precedes a painting. Tooker reflects that "the original intaglio print of *Night* (1975) was the first time that I worked completely without color. It was difficult, but I did another intaglio afterward—*Repose* (1976)." His drawing style for the final proofs for his lithographs is more dependent upon shading and therefore closer to that of his paintings than are his working drawings. However, he still does not consider working on lithographs a completely satisfactory experience, nor does he accept drawing for its own sake as a desirable goal. Painting remains his love.

*fig. 32*

There is a mystique about drawing in Western culture, especially since the Renaissance. The ability of the artist to portray reality visually and to evoke an emotive response has been likened to the power inherent in an almighty God. This "derived from a belief that the creativity of the artist re-enacted the creation of the world."(2) Today we continue to acknowledge the power of preliminary drawings. We see them as giving us insight into an artist's creative powers as well as into aspects of his personality or what earlier times referred to as his "soul". We continue to believe that preliminary drawings reveal the essence of a creative idea, that we can participate directly in the artist's creativity by responding to the drawing as visual thinking on paper. Whatever the impetus for the creation of the drawings and the function they serve the artist, to the viewer, working drawings present an opportunity to participate in an artist's creative process. Viewing them may even be considered a glimpse into the very mechanism of "artistic genius".

These perceptions and feelings about working drawings are shared by many artists even in the twentieth century. However, regardless of the kind of mystique we attribute to his drawings, the artist sees his own working drawings as very personal and revealing. This is certainly true of George Tooker. "Drawings are like an old hat or an old shoe. They are a part of me, a part of my past, a part of my thoughts. They are very private, intimate and self-revealing. Because they are very personal, they were never meant to be seen by anyone other than myself."

Tooker's working drawings have never been exhibited before, although a number were reproduced in Thomas Garver's 1985 monograph of his complete works. Tooker has decided to let them be exhibited in this instance only because they are to be in an educational setting within a university museum.

In working drawings, forms are often delineated only by sketchy lines suggestive of shapes, space, light and movement; grids and diagonals are drawn to outline a plan for the compositional structure, and various colors are daubed, tried out or over-painted, or swabs of samples are painted next to each other. The drawings show the painstaking exploration of ideas in the very early formative stages of a work. They reveal the process of experimentation in working out technical problems faced in the development of the painting. At other times they are mere doodlings, jottings of ideas, which may have already or will become the sources and inspiration for new works. They may be recordings of actual events, real people, objects or landscapes drawn from the artist's experience or imagination which may reappear in various guises in the finished works. Frequently the artist is reluctant to put such raw, unresolved, intensely personal works under the scrutiny of the public used to looking at his finished, polished works.

The subjectivity and feeling of immediacy of working drawings makes them precious. There is a sense of the familiar combined with a feeling of the sacred about them that promulgates an appreciation and an understanding on many levels when we view and study them. They have an inherent ability to evoke a perception of a universality of vision and experience which transcends time and place. George Tooker's working drawings do make us witnesses to his creative process and provide us with an insight into not only his thinking but his emotive life as well. Participating in Tooker's vision as revealed in his working drawings enriches our understanding of ourselves, our fellow man and our times. We are left with a deeper appreciation of the intensity of feeling balanced with the philosophical construct and intellectual integrity bearing testimony to the creative control he has achieved in his art.



(1) All of George Tooker's comments in this essay are based upon the author's interview with him on July 8, 1987.

(2) Susan Lambert, *Reading Drawings*, Pantheon Books, New York, 1984, p.9.

# ILLUSTRATIONS

PHOTO CREDITS:

| | |
|---|---|
| Black/white photography: | Michael Kemsley<br>University of Vermont Photo Services<br>Burlington, Vermont |
| Color Photography: | Barbara Leslie<br>Glenn Moody Photographers<br>Burlington, Vermont |
| Color Separations: | Champlain Color Corporation<br>Burlington, Vermont |
| George Roos: | Study for *Subway*, Study for *Lovers I* |

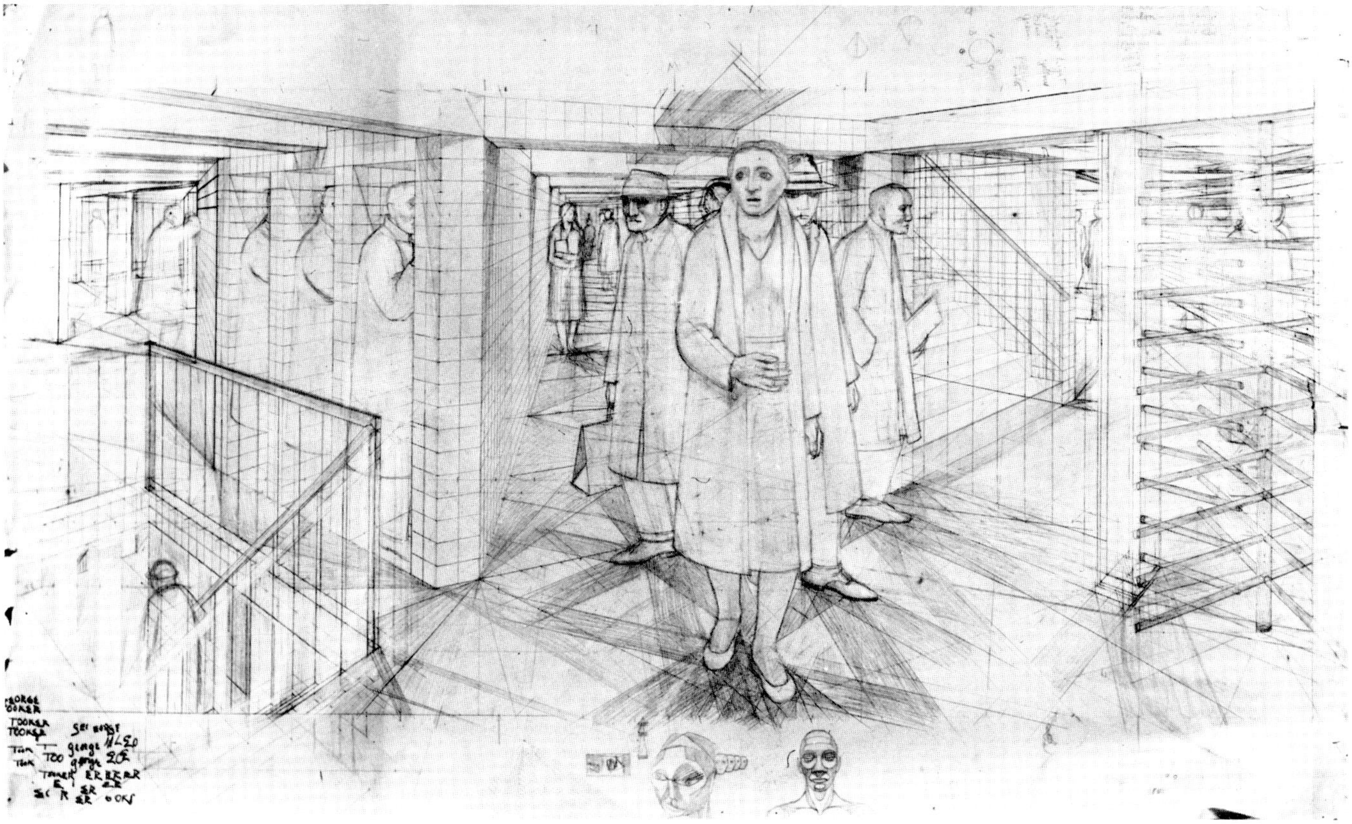

8

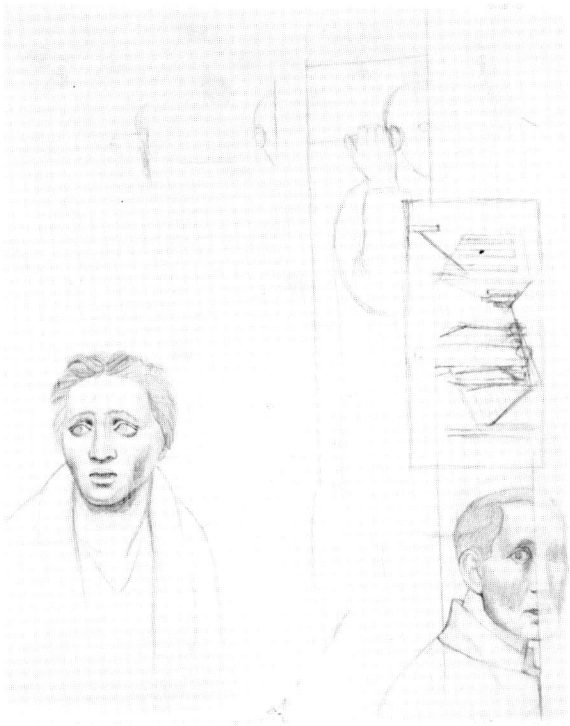

9

10

18

Studies
for *Subway*
1950

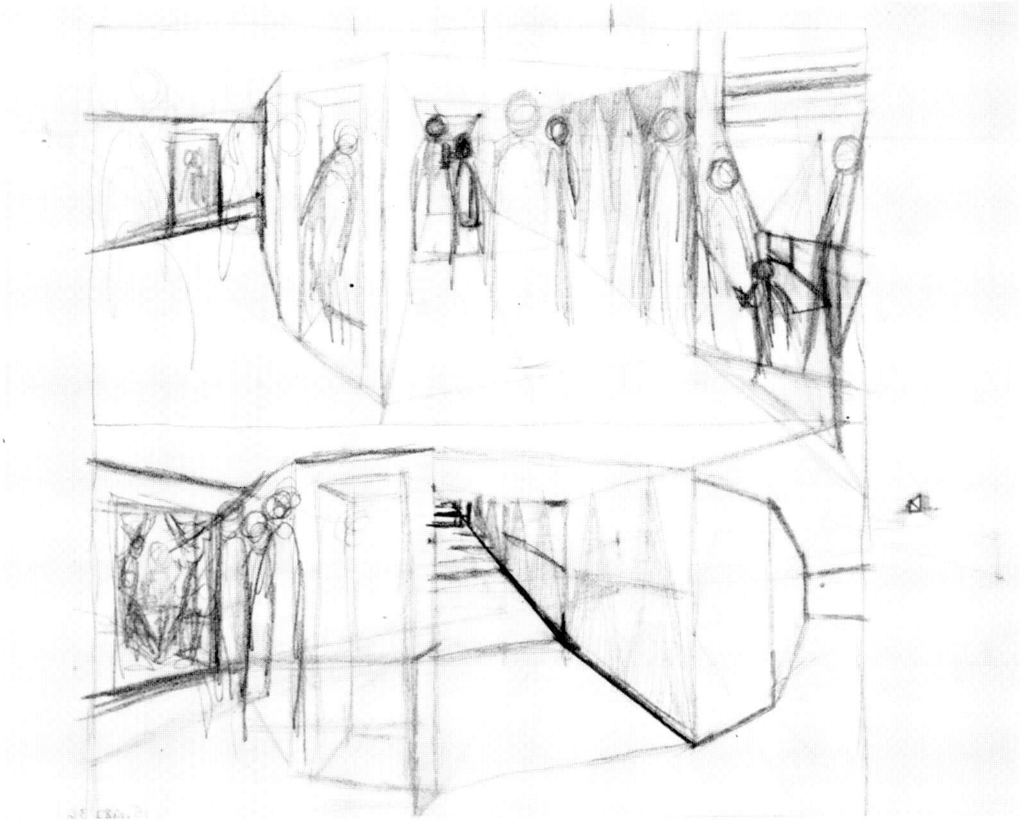

11

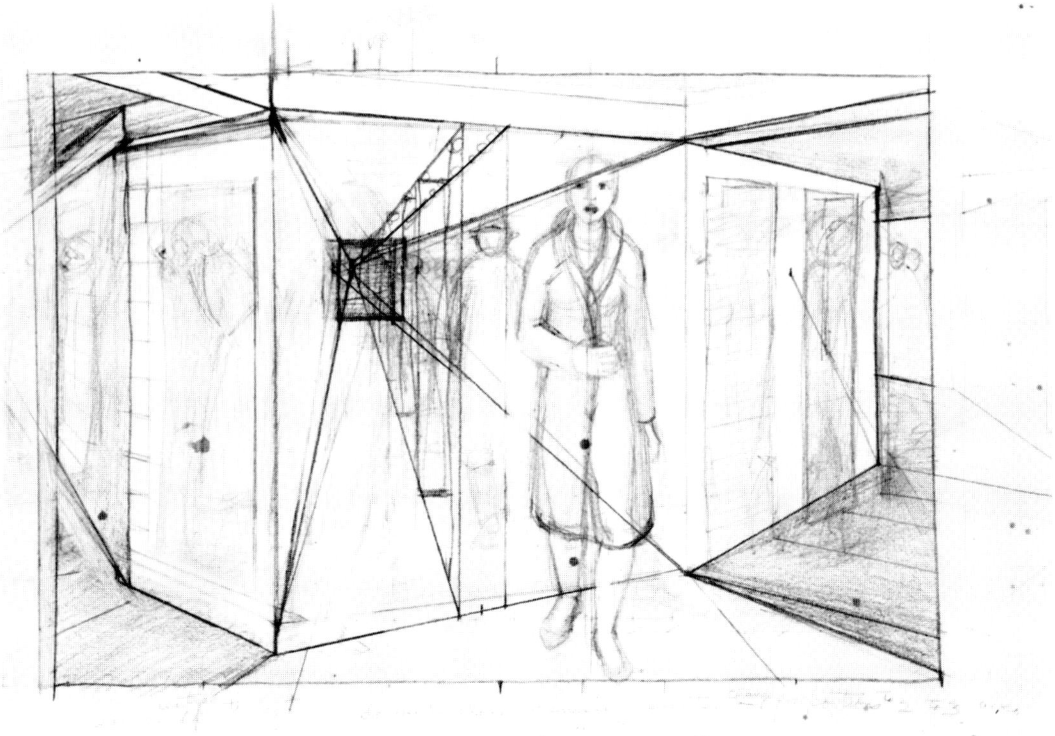

12



Studies
for *Subway*
1950

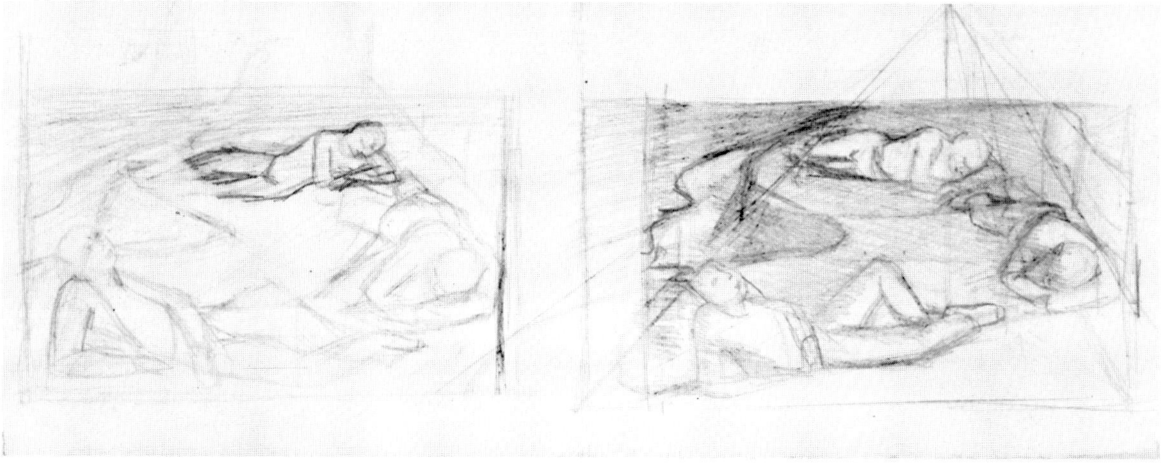

13

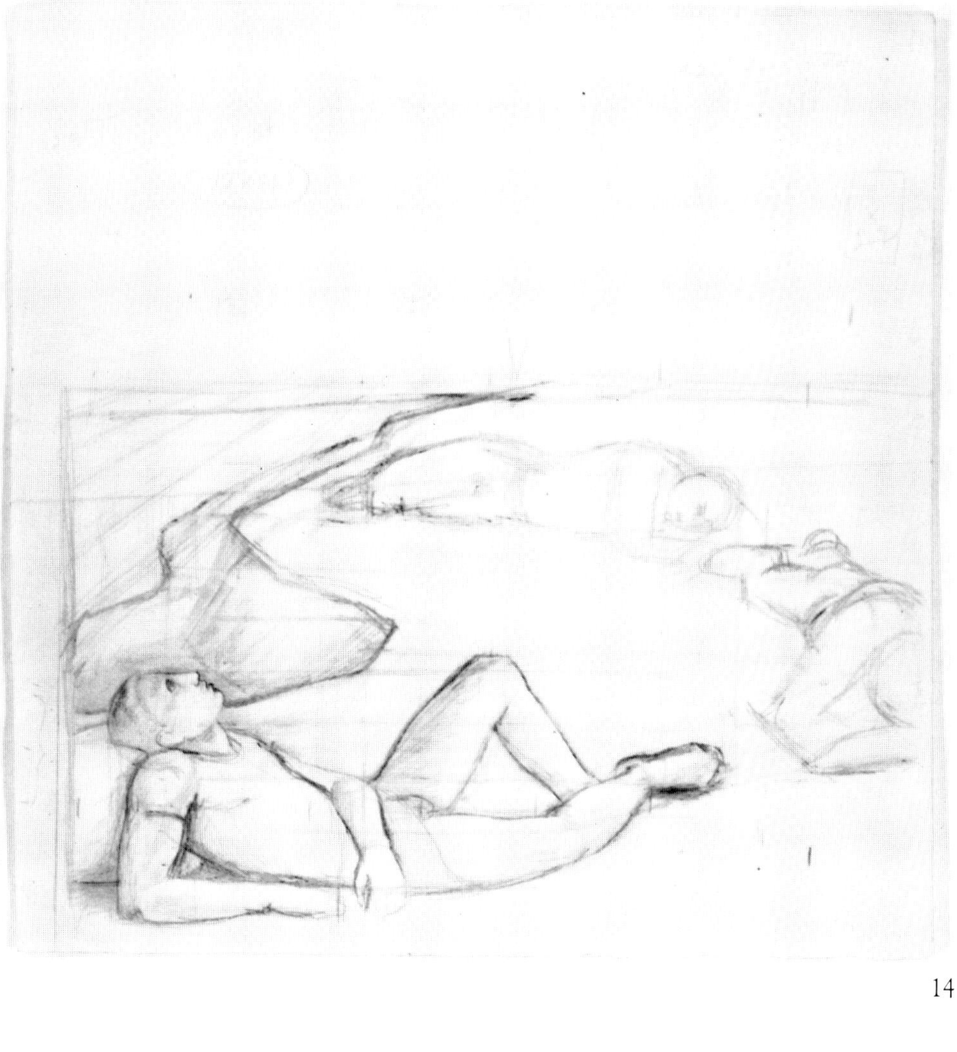

14



Studies
for
*Sleepers I*
1951

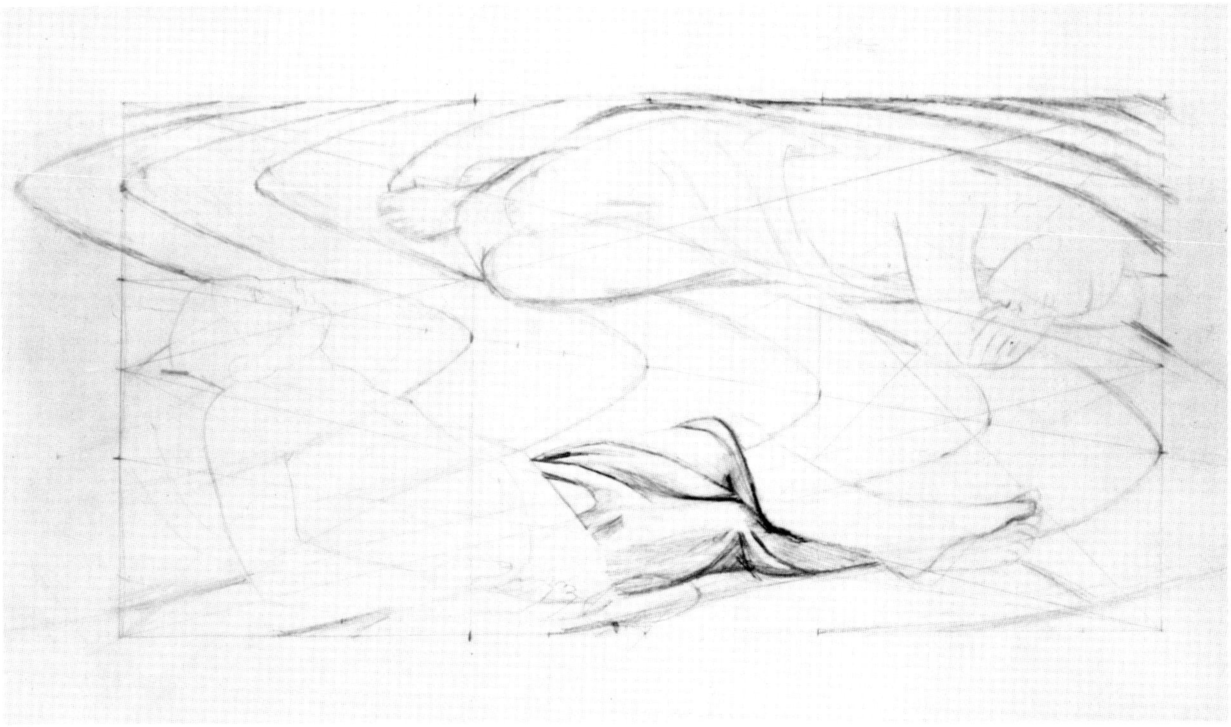

15

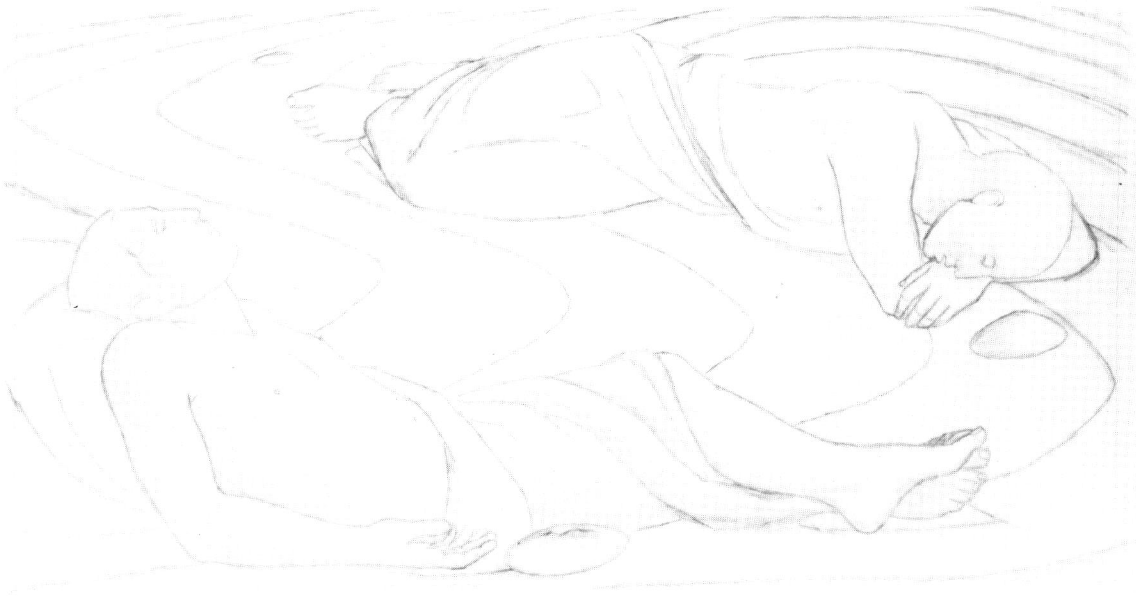

16

21

Studies
for
*Sleepers IV*
1978

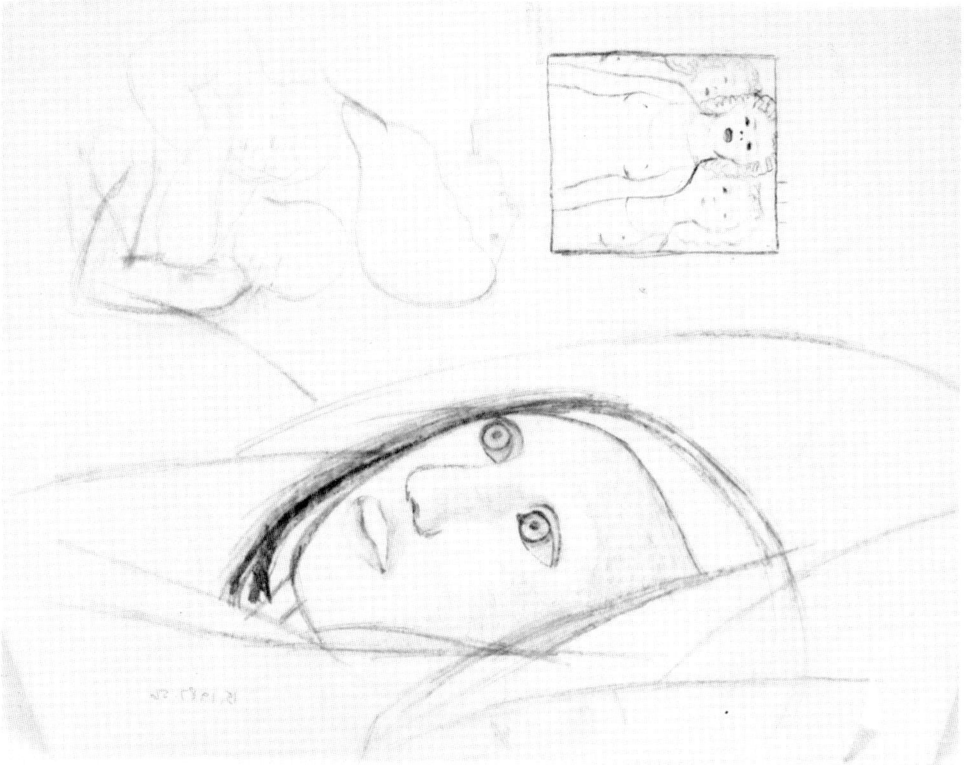

17

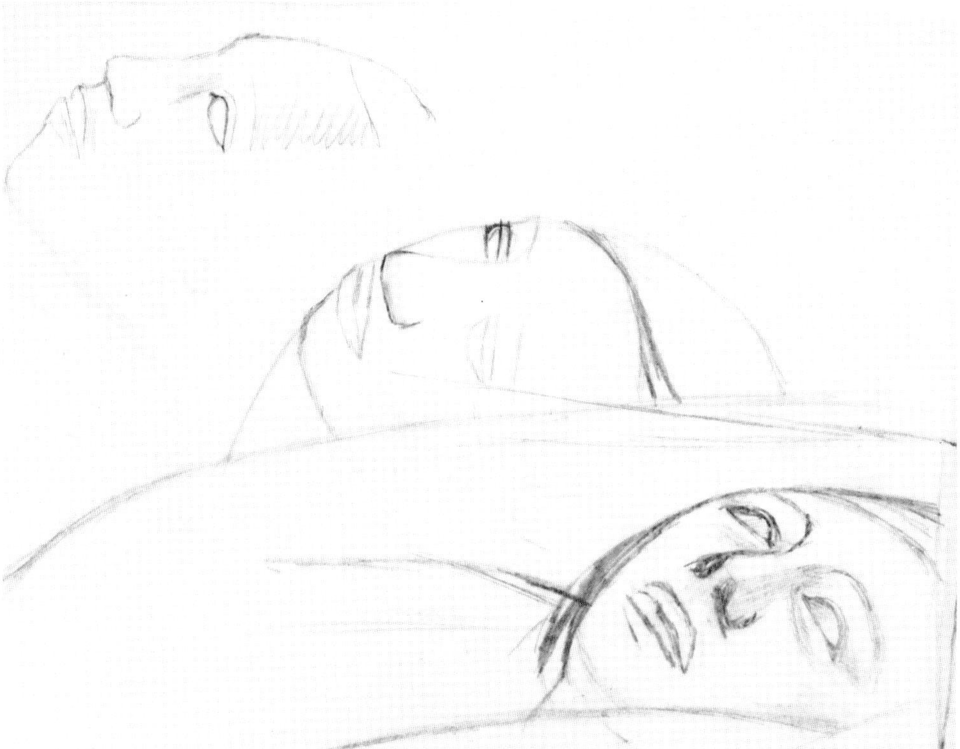

18



Studies
for
*Sleepers II*
1957

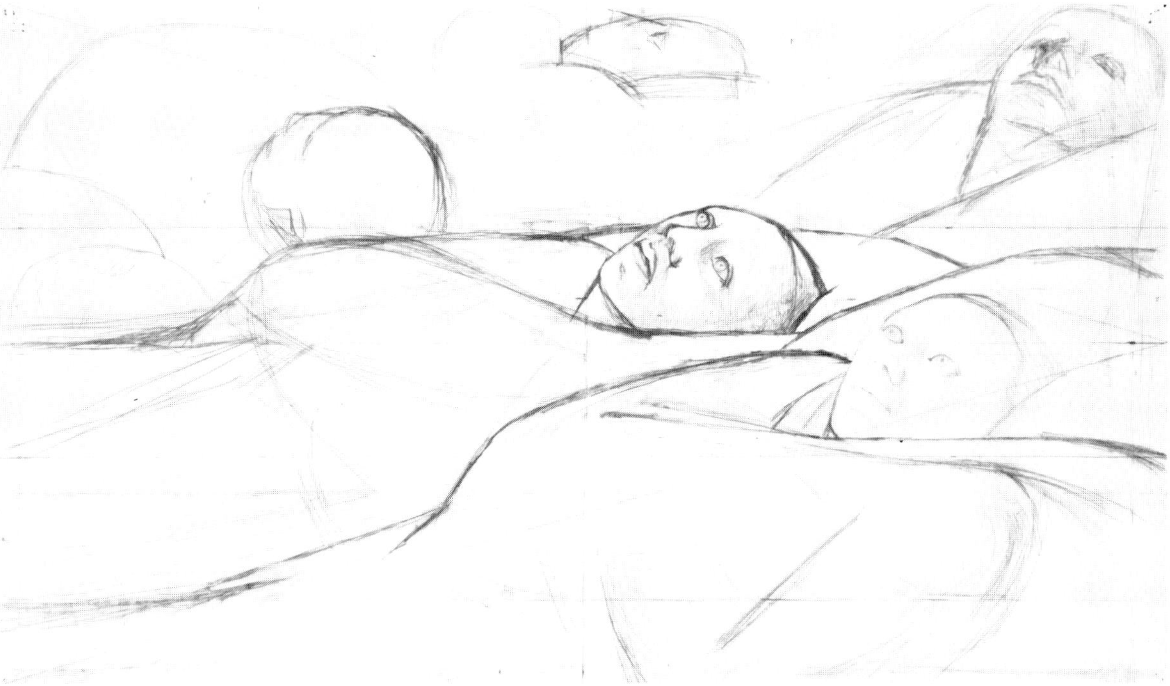

19

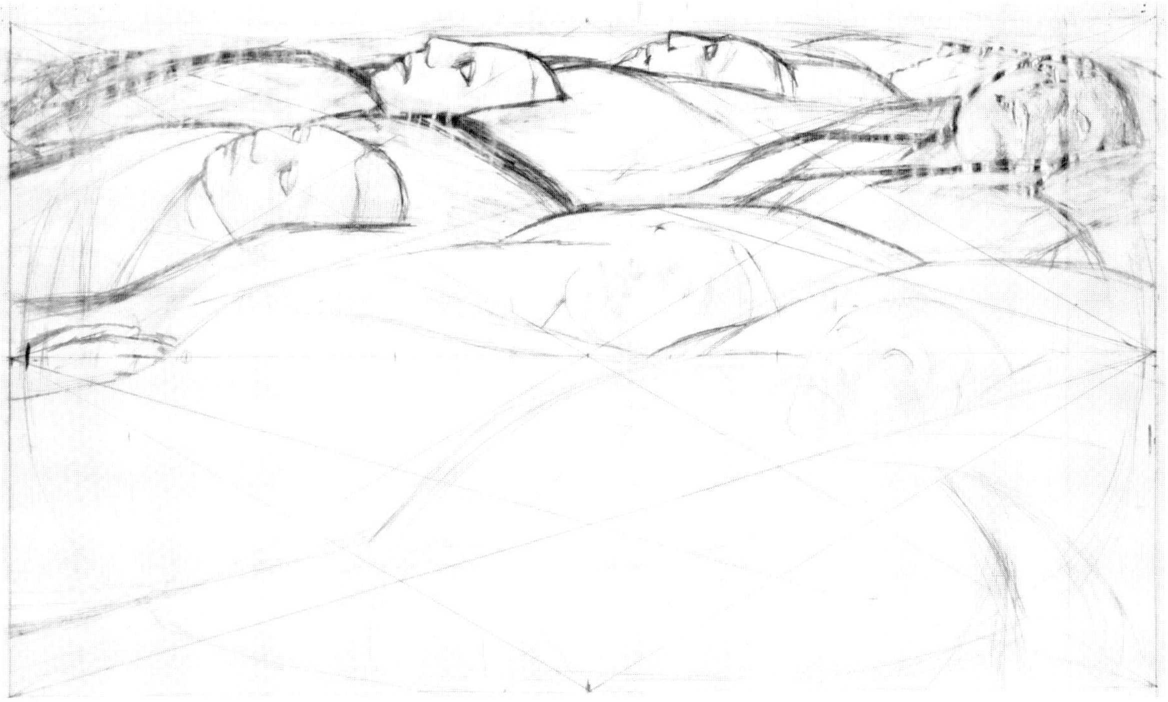

20

23

Studies
for
*Sleepers II*
1957

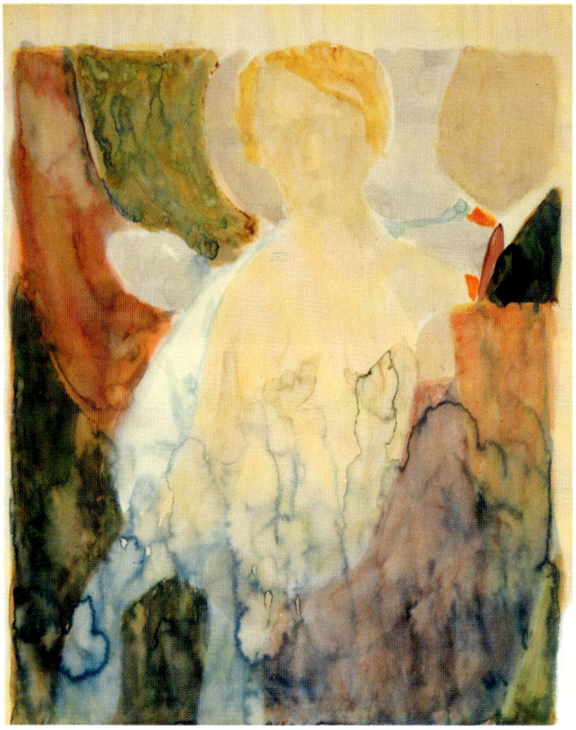

21

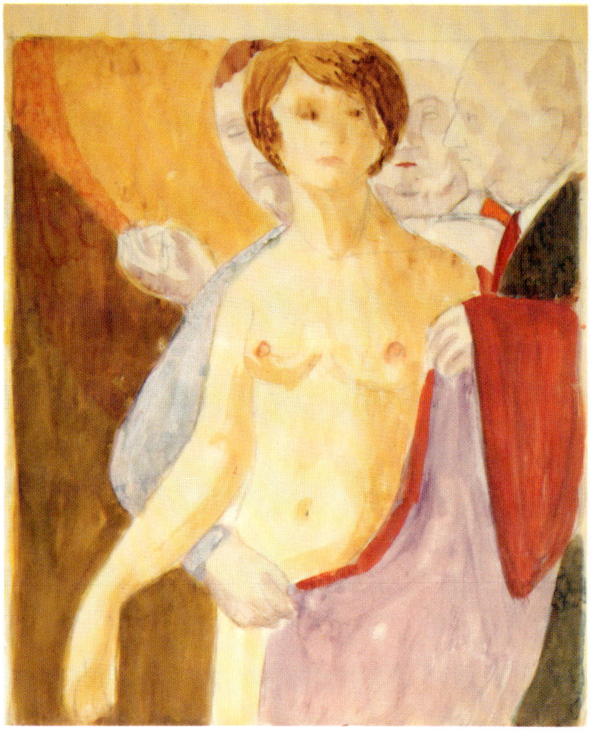

22



Studies
for
*Toilette*
1962

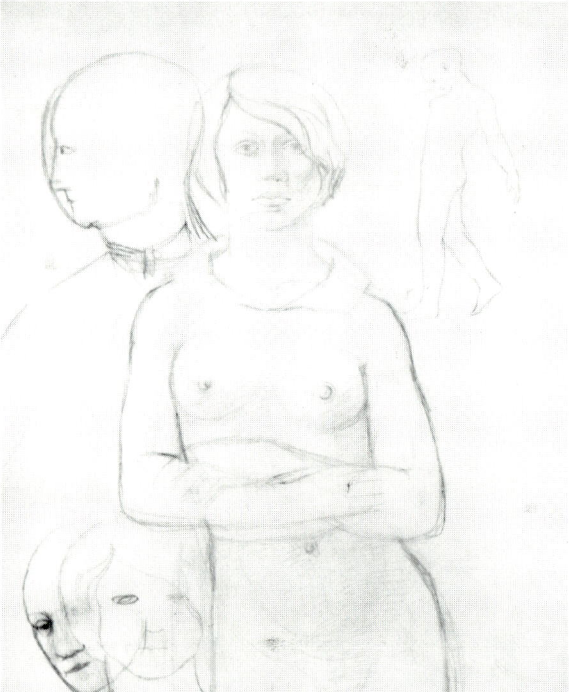

23

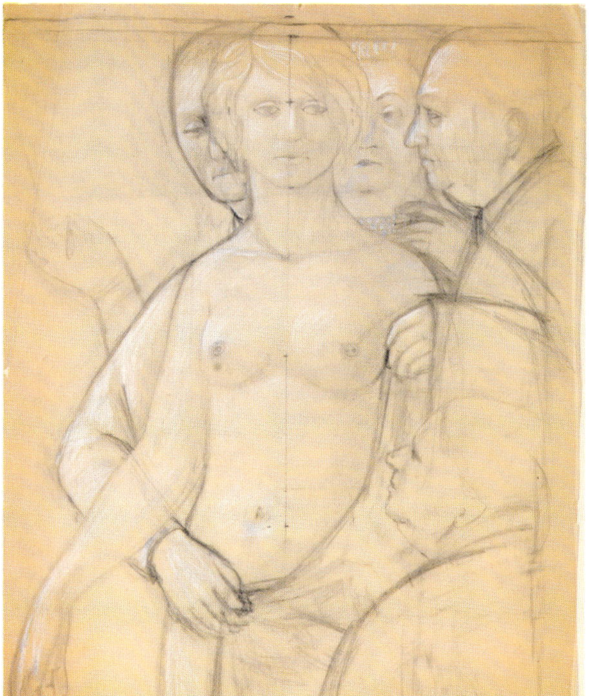

24

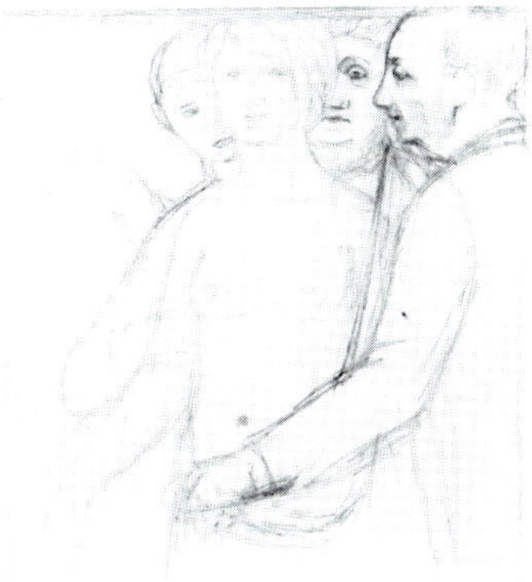

25

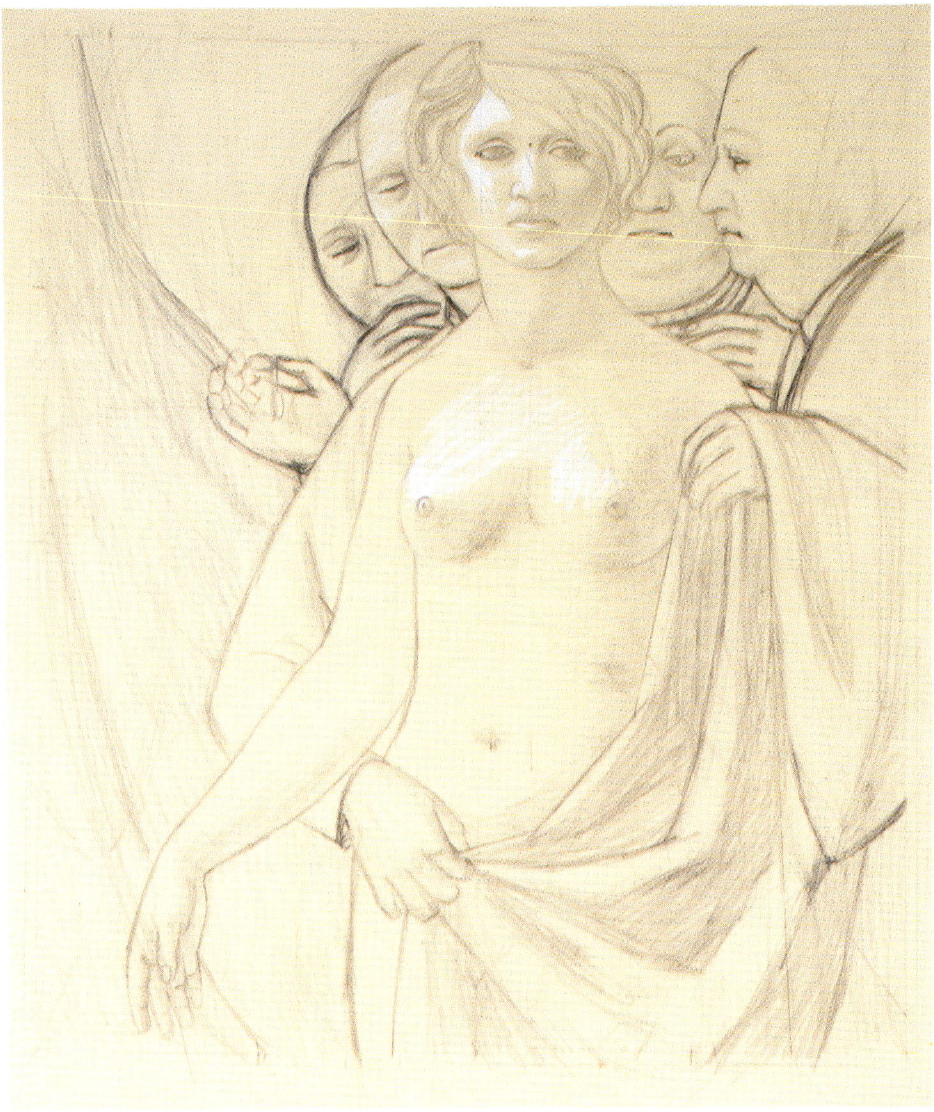

26

25

Studies
for
*Toilette*
1962

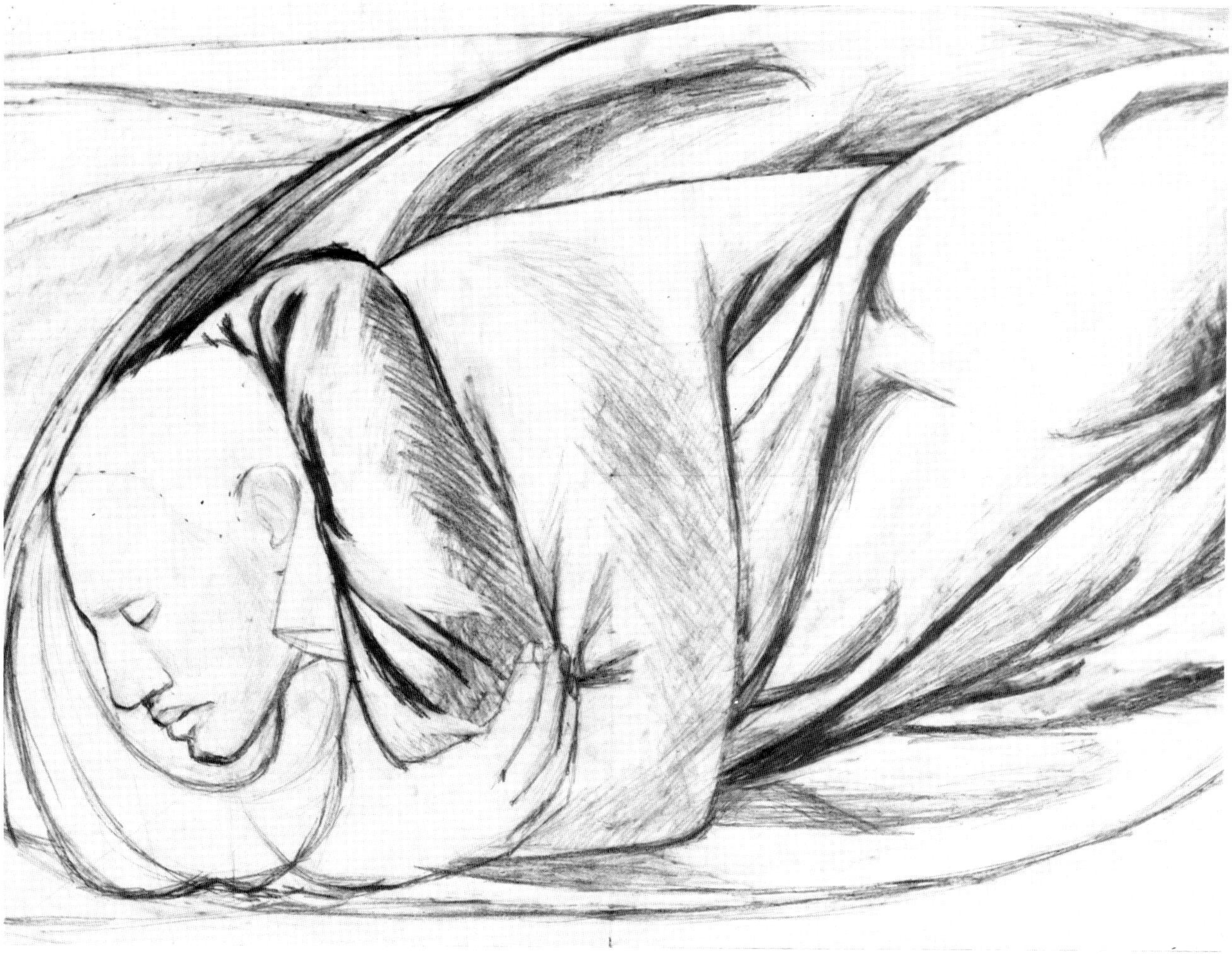



26

Study
for
*Lovers I*
1959

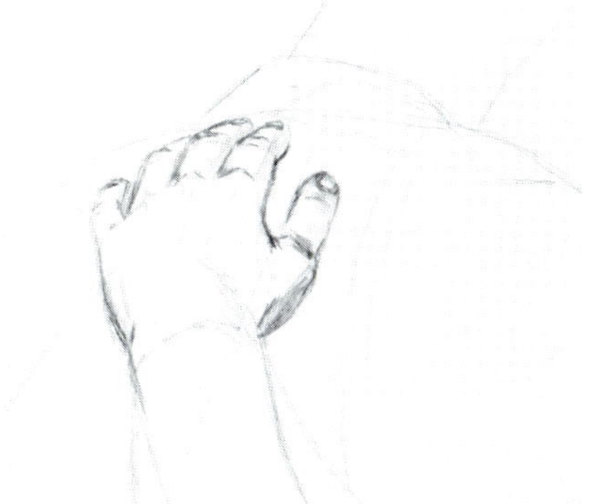

28

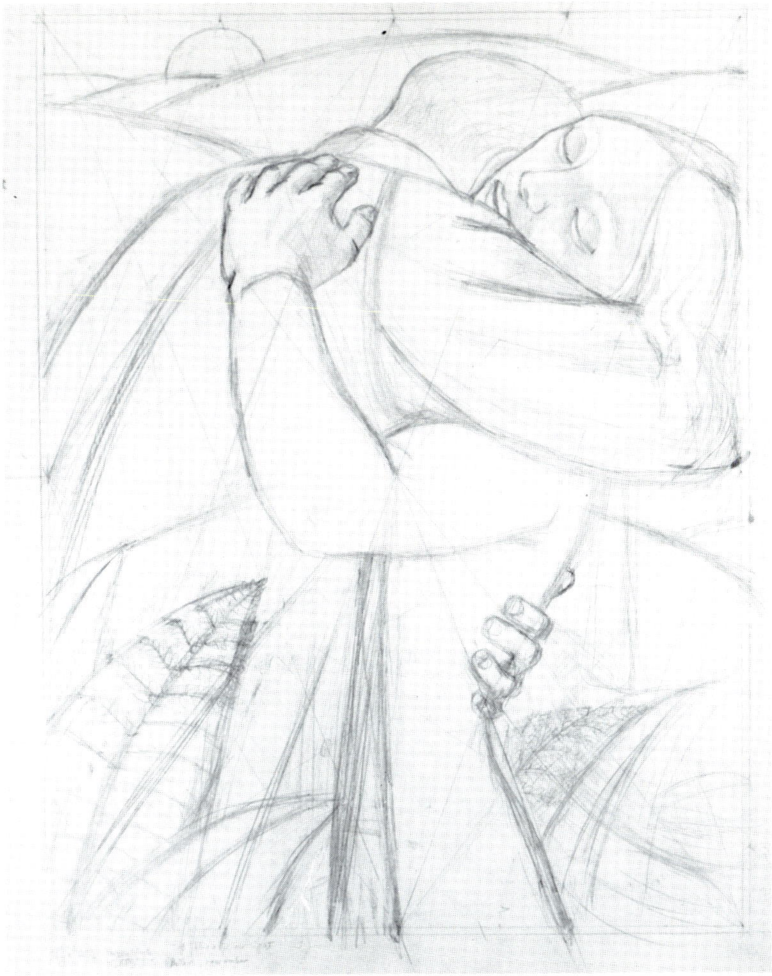

29

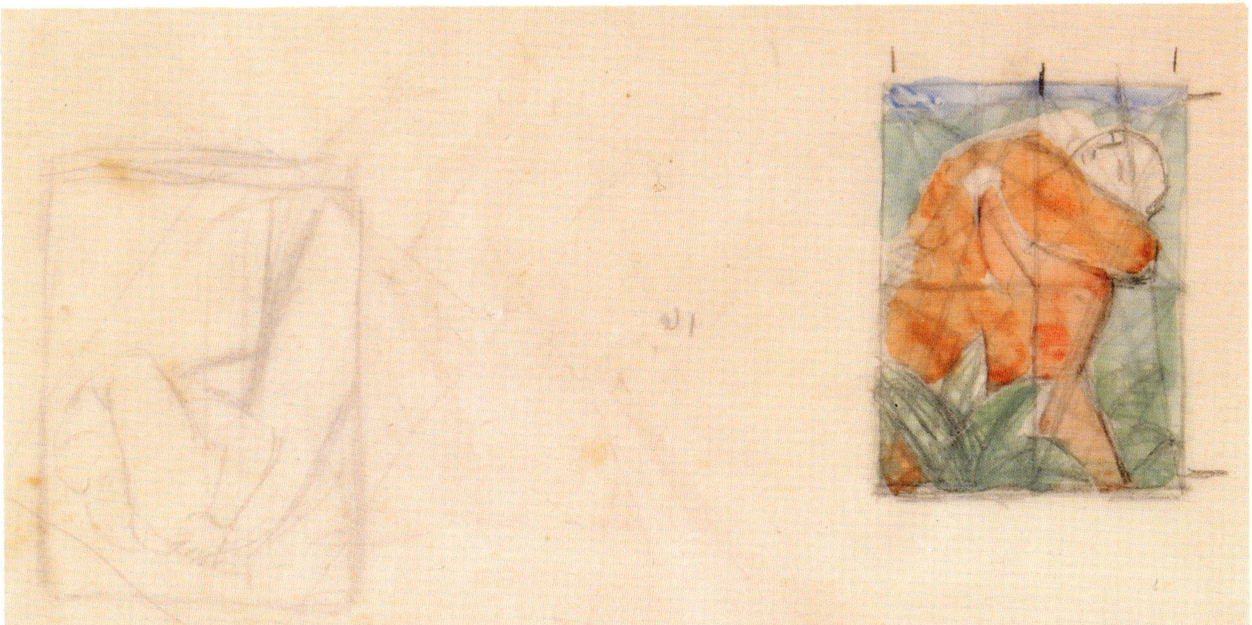

30

27

Studies
for
*Embrace I*
1979

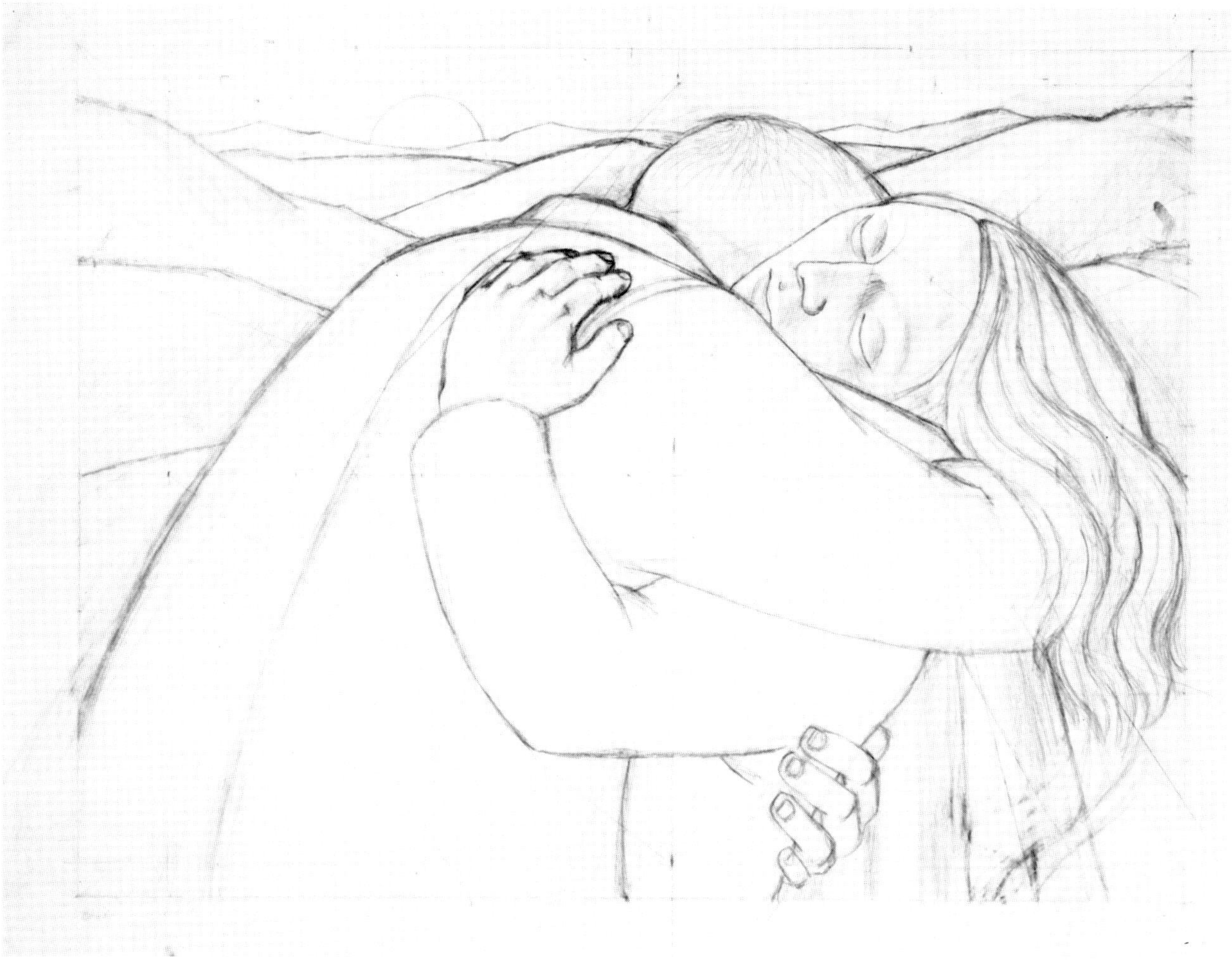



28

Study
for
*Embrace II*
1981

# CHECKLIST OF THE EXHIBITION

*Asterisked items are illustrated in the catalogue.

Unless otherwise noted, all items have been lent by the artist.

Studies for SELF-PORTRAIT (1947)
Gouache and graphite on watercolor paper (folded)
Sheet 28.5 × 39.6 cm

Study for SELF-PORTRAIT (1947)
Graphite on tracing paper
Sheet 21.6 × 27.8 cm

Study for FESTA (1948)
Graphite on paper
49.5 × 37.5 cm

Study for FESTA (1948)
Graphite and white wash on brown paper
54.5 × 44.5 cm, sheet 61 × 46 cm

Study for FESTA (1948)
Watercolor and graphite on paper
21.5 × 35 cm

BATHERS (BATH HOUSES) (1950)
Egg tempera on panel
51.4 × 38.7 cm
Private Collection

Study for BATHERS (1950)
Graphite on paper
51 × 38 cm, sheet 70.5 × 53.5 cm

* Study for THE SUBWAY (1950)
Graphite on paper
Sheet 46.5 × 91.5 cm

* Study for THE SUBWAY (1950)
Graphite on heavy white paper
15.4 × 23.2 cm, sheet 19 × 29 cm

* Studies for THE SUBWAY (1950)
Graphite on tracing paper
20.4 × 20.4 cm, sheet 21.6 × 27.9 cm

* Studies for THE SUBWAY (1950)
Graphite on tracing paper
Sheet 27.9 × 21.7 cm

* Studies for THE SUBWAY (1950)
Graphite on tracing paper
Sheet 27.9 × 21.7 cm

Study for SLEEPERS I (1951)
Graphite on blue paper
7.2 × 10.8 cm, sheet 10.4 × 13.7 cm

Study for SLEEPERS I (1951)
Graphite on blue paper
6.5 × 11 cm, sheet 10.4 × 13.7 cm

* Studies for SLEEPERS I (1951)
Graphite on folded white paper
Sheet 10 × 26 cm

* Study for SLEEPERS I (1951)
Graphite on white paper, recto & verso
17 × 28 cm, sheet 29.5 × 29.5 cm

WINDOW I (1955)
Egg tempera on panel
60.3 × 40.6 cm
Walker Art Center, Minneapolis, MN

* Study for WINDOW I (1955)
Graphite and color wash on tracing paper
6.5 × 6.3 cm, sheet 7.8 × 6.6 cm

* Study for WINDOW I (1955)
Graphite on tracing paper
15.7 × 16 cm, sheet 17.7 × 21.5 cm

* Study for WINDOW I (1955)
Graphite on tracing paper
16.5 × 12 cm, sheet 22.8 × 22.5 cm

* Studies for WINDOW I (1955)
Colored pencil and graphite on tracing paper
Sheet 29.8 × 13.5 cm

* Study for WINDOW 1 (1955)
Graphite, white conté crayon, pastel, and ink on buff paper
52 × 43 cm, sheet 62.2 × 47 cm

Study for GOVERNMENT BUREAU (1956)
Graphite, white chalk and brown wash on buff paper
59 × 76.5 cm, sheet 66 × 83 cm

Study for GOVERNMENT BUREAU (1956)
Graphite on paper
Sheet 21.4 × 27.9 cm

Study for GOVERNMENT BUREAU (1956)
Graphite on paper
Sheet 22.5 × 21.5 cm

* Studies for SLEEPERS II (1957) and ENTERTAINERS (1959-60)
Graphite on tracing paper
Sheet 22.9 × 29.7 cm

* Study for SLEEPERS II (1957)
Graphite on tracing paper
Sheet 30 × 23 cm

* Study for SLEEPERS II (1957)
Graphite on paper
40.7 × 71.2 cm

* Study for SLEEPERS II (1957)
Graphite on white paper
41 × 71.5 cm, sheet 46 × 76.5

Study for SLEEPERS II (1957)
Graphite and red conté crayon on buff paper
30.5 × 53 cm, sheet 41 × 76.5 cm

* Study for LOVERS I (1959)
Graphite on paper
Sheet 45.9 × 60.8 cm

Study for LOVERS I (1959)
Graphite on tracing paper
12.2 × 16.3 cm, sheet 22.9 × 30.3 cm

Study for LOVERS I (1959)
Graphite on tracing paper
13 × 18 cm, sheet 23 × 30.3 cm

Study for LOVERS I (1959)
Graphite on tracing paper
12.6 × 16.9 cm, sheet 22.9 × 30.2 cm

Study for LOVERS I (1959)
Color wash on tracing paper
12.5 × 18.3 cm, sheet 22.5 × 29.8 cm

Study for THE WAITING ROOM (1959)
Graphite on buff paper
61 × 76.5 cm, sheet 69.5 × 91.5 cm

Studies for THE WAITING ROOM (1959)
Graphite on paper
Sheet 21.4 × 27.9 cm

Study for LOVERS II (1960)
Graphite on buff paper
56 × 65 cm, sheet 61 × 72.6 cm

Study for LOVERS II (1960)
Graphite on paper
11.2 × 14 cm, sheet 14.6 × 18.5 cm

Study for LOVERS II (1960)
Graphite on tracing paper
9.7 × 11.7 cm, sheet 35.3 × 27.9 cm

Studies for LOVERS II (1960)
1 graphite with 4 color wash studies on tracing paper
Sheet 35 × 27.5 cm

Studies for LOVERS II (first study) (1960)
Graphite on tracing paper
Sheet 22 × 23 cm

Studies for LOVERS II (1960)
Graphite on tracing paper
Sheet 19.4 × 13.8 cm (irregular)

Study for LOVERS II (1960)
Graphite on tracing paper
Sheet 9.5 × 11.4 cm

MEADOW I, 1960–61
Egg tempera on panel
55.9 cm × 38.1 cm
Steven and Channa Wintner

Study for MEADOW I (1960–61)
Graphite on drafting paper, verso red pigment overall
51 × 75.5 cm sheet 64.5 × 83 cm

Study for MEADOW I (1960–61)
Graphite on gray paper
Sheet 12.5 × 17.8 cm

Study for MEADOW I (1960–61)
Graphite and color wash on tracing paper
18.3 × 30 cm, sheet 22.5 × 29.9 cm

Study for MEADOW I (1960–61)
Graphite on tracing paper
17 × 23.5 cm, sheet 23 × 30.3 cm

Study for MEADOW I (1960–61)
Graphite on tracing paper
15 × 21 cm, sheet 23 × 34 cm

Study for MEADOW I (1960–61)
Graphite on tracing paper
17.5 × 24.2 cm, sheet 22.9 × 30.3 cm

Study for MEADOW I (1960–61)
Graphite on tracing paper
Sheet 33 × 23 cm

Study for MEADOW I (1960–61)
Graphite on tracing paper, recto & verso
Sheet 30.3 × 23 cm

Study for MEADOW I (1960–61)
Graphite on tracing paper
Sheet 27.9 × 35.3 cm

Studies for MIRROR I (1962)
Graphite and white conté crayon on tracing paper
Sheet 28 × 35 cm

Study for MIRROR I (1962)
Graphite on tracing paper
15.5 × 14 cm, sheet 28 × 21.4 cm

Study for MIRROR I (1962)
Graphite on vellum, verso black crayon
50.8 × 40.6 cm, sheet 76.9 × 64.5 cm

Study for MIRROR I (1962)
Graphite on buff paper
51.2 × 55.8 cm, sheet 56.7 × 53.2 cm

* Study for TOILETTE (1962)
Graphite with white conté crayon on buff paper
54.5 × 45.7 cm, sheet 63 × 53.6 cm

* Studies for TOILETTE (1962)
Graphite on tracing paper
Sheet 35.3 × 28 cm

* Study for TOILETTE (1962)
Graphite on paper
13.8 × 11.6 cm, sheet 18.4 × 14.8 cm

* Study for TOILETTE (1962)
Color wash on tracing paper
32.6 × 25.8 cm, sheet 35 × 27.7 cm

* Study for TOILETTE (1962)
Color wash on tracing paper
32.8 × 27 cm, sheet 35 × 27.7 cm

* Study for TOILETTE (1962)
Graphite with white conté crayon on tracing paper
33.6 × 26.5 cm, sheet 35.6 × 27.9 cm

Study for NIGHT I (1963)
Graphite on buff paper
45.3 × 57.8 cm, sheet 47.1 × 53.7 cm

MIRROR II, (1964)
Egg tempera on panel
50.8 × 50.8 cm
Addison Gallery of American Art,
Phillips Academy,
Andover MA. Gift of R. H. Donnelley Erdman

Study for MIRROR II (1964)
Graphite and color wash on tan paper
50.7 × 50.6 cm, sheet 54.5 × 56.3 cm

ODALISQUE (1967)
Egg tempera on panel
61 × 45.7 cm
Private collection

Study for ODALISQUE (1967)
Graphite and watercolor on buff paper
Sheet 66.8 × 65 cm

Study for ODALISQUE (1967)
Graphite on vellum, verso red pigment overall
61 × 45.5 cm, sheet 92.3 × 70 cm

GYPSIES (1968)
Egg tempera on panel
45.7 × 61 cm
Mr. and Mrs. Joel W. Harnett

Studies for GYPSIES (1968)
Graphite & color wash on tracing paper, recto & verso
Sheet 21.5 × 27.8 cm

Study for GYPSIES (1968)
Graphite and color wash on tracing paper
10 × 10 cm, sheet 14.9 × 22.6

Study for GYPSIES (1968)
Graphite and color crayon on tracing paper
9.5 × 9.5 cm, sheet 12.5 × 14.2 (irregular)

Studies for GYPSIES (1968)
Graphite on tracing paper
Sheet 21.5 × 13.8 cm (irregular)

Study for GYPSIES (1968)
Graphite on buff paper
60.5 × 59.7 cm, sheet 66.8 × 67 cm

Study for SELF-PORTRAIT (1969)
Graphite on buff paper
61 × 49 cm, sheet 70.7 × 55 cm

Study for MIRROR IV (1976–79)
Graphite on tracing paper
16 × 18.5 cm, sheet 30 × 22.8 cm

Study for MIRROR IV (1976–79)
Graphite on tracing paper
19.7 × 16.5 cm, sheet 30 × 22.8 cm

Study for MIRROR IV (1976–79)
Graphite on white paper
60.8 × 51.4 cm, sheet 67.2 × 53.6 cm

Study for ORANT (APPLAUSE) (1977)
Graphite on tracing paper, verso red pigment overall
59.5 × 39 cm, sheet 75.7 × 45.7 cm

Study for ORANT (1977)
Graphite on buff paper
Sheet 74.5 × 45.5 cm

Study for ORANT (1977)
Graphite on paper
19.5 × 21.5 cm, sheet 20.4 × 25.5 cm

Studies for ORANT (1977)
Graphite on tracing paper, displayed folded to show superimposed images
Sheet 48 × 30.3 cm

Study for ORANT (1977)
Graphite on tracing paper
19.4 × 19.1 cm, sheet 24 × 30.4 cm

Study for ORANT (1977)
Graphite on tracing paper
19.6 × 25 cm, sheet 24 × 30.4 cm

Study for MEADOW II (1977–79)
Graphite on tracing paper
20 × 14.3 cm, sheet 22.8 16.2 cm

Study for MEADOW II (1977–79)
Graphite on tracing paper
Sheet 29 × 21.6 cm, (irregular)

Study for MEADOW II (1977–79)
Graphite on drafting paper
54.2 × 36.4 cm, sheet 76.8 × 51.6 cm

Study for MEADOW II (1977–79)
Graphite and green watercolor on vellum
55.6 × 38 cm, sheet 76.7 × 50.3 cm

SLEEPERS IV (1978)
Egg tempera on panel
30.5 × 61 cm
Private collection

* Study for SLEEPERS IV (1978)
Graphite on vellum
30.5 × 60.8 cm, sheet 45.5 × 76.8 cm

* Study for SLEEPERS IV (1978)
Graphite on vellum
30.5 × 60.9 cm, sheet 46.1 × 76.9 cm

* Studies for EMBRACE I (1979)
Graphite and color wash on tracing paper
Sheet 15 × 22.6 cm

* Study for EMBRACE I (1979)
Graphite on buff paper
60.2 × 45.4, sheet 76.5 × 51.4 cm

* Study for EMBRACE I (1979)
Graphite on tracing paper
Sheet 22.5 × 30.2 cm

EMBRACE II (1981)
Egg tempera on panel
45.7 × 61 cm
Kitty and Herbert Glantz

* Study for EMBRACE II (1981)
Graphite on vellum
45.5 × 60.6 cm, sheet 63.2 × 76.7 cm

* Embrace I (LOVERS) (1982)
Lithograph
42 × 40.6 cm, sheet 42 × 51 cm
Robert Hull Fleming Musem

CORPORATE DECISION (1983)
Egg tempera on panel
45.7 × 61 cm
Frank Mainzer

Study for CORPORATE DECISION (1983)
Graphite on vellum
44 × 59.8 cm, sheet 50 × 62 cm

Study for CORPORATE DECISION (1983)
Graphite and white conté crayon on vellum
34 × 60 cm, sheet 52.5 × 62 cm

Studies for CORPORATE DECISION (1983)
Graphite on tracing paper
Sheet 22.8 × 30.5 cm

Study for EMBRACE III (1983)
Graphite on white paper
40.5 × 48.1 cm, sheet 43 × 50.8 cm

Study for EMBRACE II (1984 lithograph)
Graphite on paperboard
30.5 × 40.5 cm, sheet 35.1 × 45.7 cm

Study for EMBRACE II (1984 lithograph)
Graphite on paperboard
40.5 × 48.5 cm, sheet 43 × 51 cm

SELF-PORTRAIT (1984)
Lithograph
21.5 × 20 cm, sheet 46 × 35.5 cm
Robert Hull Fleming Museum

EMBRACE IV (1984)
Egg tempera on panel
40.6 × 48.9 cm
Private Collection

Study for EMBRACE IV (1984)
Graphite and crayon on paper
41.5 × 48.5 cm, sheet 45.3 × 51 cm

GEORGE TOOKER (1985)
David Teplica
Gelatine silver print—artist's proof
24.3 × 18.8 cm, sheet 45.5 × 37.8 cm

Study for EMBRACE OF PEACE (1986)
Graphite on vellum
45.5 × 71 cm, sheet 62.3 × 79.7 cm

WINDOW 1987 (1987)
Egg tempera on panel
Dimensions unknown
Lent by the artist

Study for WINDOW 1987 (1987)
Graphite on tracing paper
22.5 × 21 cm, sheet 22.5 × 30 cm

Study for WINDOW 1987 (1987)
Graphite with wash on vellum
27.8 × 20.9 cm, sheet 43.3 × 27.8 cm

Study for WINDOW 1987 (1987)
Graphite on vellum
24 × 24 cm, sheet 27.8 × 43.2 cm

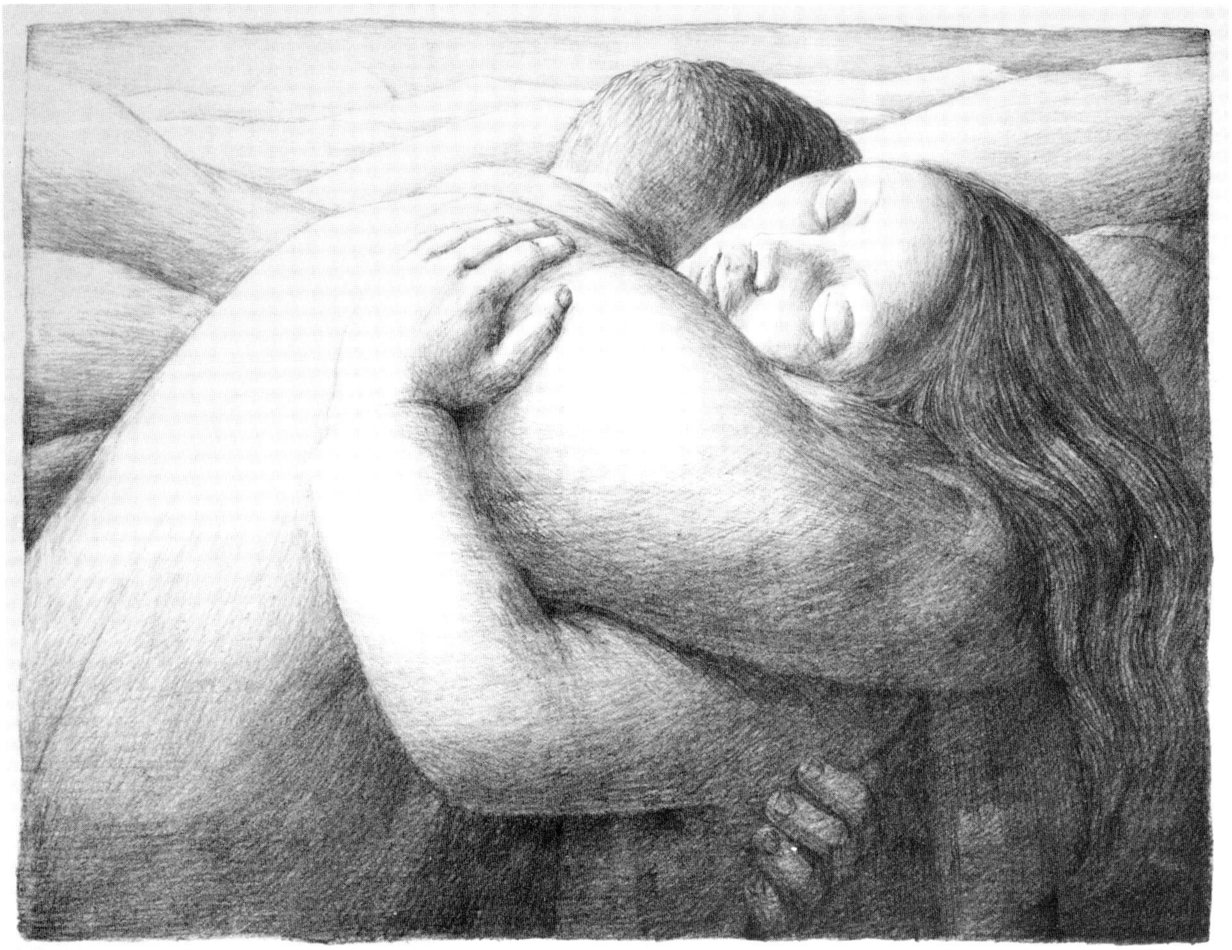

32



*Embrace I*
lithograph
1982

# BIOGRAPHY AND EXHIBITION HISTORY

## GEORGE CLAIR TOOKER

| | |
|---|---|
| August 5, 1920 | Born Brooklyn, New York<br>Attended High School in Bellport,<br>Long Island, New York |
| 1938 | Graduated from Phillips Academy,<br>Andover, Massachusetts |
| 1942 | Graduated from Harvard University,<br>B.A. English Literature, Cambridge,<br>Massachusetts |
| 1943–45 | Studied at Art Students League,<br>New York City |
| 1945–late 1950's | Lived and worked in New York City |
| 1960 | Moved to Vermont |
| 1965–68 | Taught at Art Students League |
| 1968–74 | Lived in Malaga, Spain, six months of the year |
| 1976 | Converted to Catholicism |
| 1974–present | Lives and works in Hart-land, Vermont |

## ONE-ARTIST EXHIBITIONS

1951
Edwin Hewitt Gallery, New York

1967
"George Tooker: Paintings and Drawings." Jaffe-Friede Gallery, Hopkins Center, Dartmouth College, Hanover, New Hampshire
Catalogue

1974–75
"George Tooker: Paintings 1947–1973." Fine Arts Museums of San Francisco, California, Palace of the Legion of Honor, San Francisco. Also exhibited at Museum of Contemporary Art, Chicago; Whitney Museum of Art, New York; Indianapolis Museum of Art; Indianapolis.
Catalogue by Thomas H. Garver.

1985
"George Tooker: Paintings 1948–1985." Marisa Del Re Gallery, New York. February 6–March 2.

1987
"George Tooker: Working Drawings," Robert Hull Fleming Museum, University of Vermont, Burlington, Vermont.

1987
"George Tooker: Paintings," Gibbes Gallery, Charlotte, South Carolina.

## GROUP EXHIBITIONS

1944
"28th Annual Exhibition: Brooklyn Society of Artists." Brooklyn Museum, Brooklyn, NY.

1946
"Fifteen Americans." The Museum of Modern Art, New York.

1947
"Annual Exhibition of Contemporary American Painting." Whitney Museum of American Art, New York.
Tooker also exhibited in the Annuals of 1948, 1949, 1952, 1953, 1955, 1956, 1957, 1958, 1961, 1963, 1965, 1967, and 1969.

1951
"22nd Biennial Exhibition of Contemporary American Oil Paintings." Corcoran Gallery of Art, Washington, D.C.
Tooker also exhibited in the Biennial of 1963.

1955
"The New Decade: 35 American Painters and Sculptors." Whitney Museum of American Art, New York. Also exhibited at the San Francisco Museum of Art; University of California, Los Angeles; Colorado Springs Fine Arts Center/City Art Museum of St. Louis, MO. Catalogue by John I.H. Baur.

1962
"Art: USA: Now." The Johnson Collection of Contemporary American Painting. Catalogue by Lee Nordness.

1963
"Painting and Drawing the Nude, Part II: The Female." The Banfer Gallery, New York.

1969
"Human Concern, Personal Torment: The Grotesque in American Art." Whitney Museum of American Art, New York. Also exhibited at the University Art Museum, Berkeley, CA.

1982
"Realism and Realities: The Other Side of American Painting, 1940–1960." Rutgers University Art Gallery, New Brunswick, NJ. Also exhibited at Montgomery Musuem of Fine Arts, Montgomery, AL, and The Art Gallery, University of Maryland, College Park. Catalogue by Greta Berman and Jeffrey Wechsler.

1983
"Dreams and Nightmares, Utopian Visions in Modern Art," Hirshhorn Museum and Sculpture Garden, Washington, D.C.



1984
"Contemporary Artists in Vermont." Robert Hull Fleming Museum, University of Vermont, Burlington.

1985
"Surreal City, 1930–1950." Whitney Museum of American Art at Philip Morris, New York.

1987
"Modern American Realism." The Sara Roby Foundation Collection. National Museum of American Art, Washington, D.C. Catalogue by Virginia M. Mechlenburg, essay by William Kloss.

## AWARDS

1960
Grant, National Institution of Arts and Letters.

1970
Member, National Academy of Design

1983
Member, American Academy and Institute of Arts and Letters.

1983
Governor's Award for Excellence in the Arts, Vermont Council on the Arts.

## PUBLIC COLLECTIONS

Addison Gallery of American Art, Phillips Academy, Andover, Massachusetts
The Brooklyn Museum of Art, Brooklyn
Hood Museum of Art, Dartmouth College, Hanover, New Hampshire
The Metropolitan Museum of Art, New York
Museum of Contemporary Art, Chicago
The Museum of Modern Art, New York
National Academy of Design, New York
National Museum of American Art, Smithsonian Institute, Washington, D.C.
The New York Historical Society, New York
Walker Art Center, Minneapolis, Minnesota
Whitney Museum of American Art, New York

## SELECTED REVIEWS

*Art Digest* 25 (March 1, 1951):24.

*Art News* 50 (March 1951):50.

*Art Digest* 29 (Janaury 1, 1955):28.

*Arts Magazine* 4 (April 1967):16.

Butler, Joseph T. "Surrealism of George Tooker." *Connoisseur* 187 (October 1974):135.

Derfner, Phyllis. *Art International* 19 (March 1975):38–40.

Gablik, Suzi. *Art News* 63 (May 1964):16.

Moorman, Margaret. *Art News* 84 (May 1985):117.

Raynor, Vivien. *Art News* 59 (April 1960):55.

__________. *Arts Magazine* 36 (May 1962):101.

__________. *The New York Times*, (February 22, 1985):C25.

Zucker, Barbara. *Art News* 74 (March 1975):109–10.

## SELECTED BIBLIOGRAPHY

Included are books, articles, and exhibition catalogues.

Baigell, Matthew. *Dictionary of American Art.* New York: Harper & Row, 1979.

Berman, Greta and Jeffery Wechsler. *Realism and Realities: The Other Side of American Painting, 1940–1960.* New Brunswick, NJ: Rutgers University Press, 1982.

*Brittanica Encyclopedia of American Art.* Chicago: Encyclopedia Brittanica, 1973.

Garver, Thomas H. *George Tooker.* San Francisco: The Fine Arts Museums of San Francisco, 1974.

Garver, Thomas H. *George Tooker.* Clarkson N. Potter, Inc./Publishers. 1985

Goodrich, Lloyd and John I.H. Baur. *American Art of Our Century.* New York: Whitney Museum of American Art, 1961.

Kirstein, Lincoln. *Symbolic Realism in American Painting, 1940–1950.* London: Institute for Contemporary Art, 1950.

Pomeroy, Ralph. "A Master of Modern Dismay." *New Lugano Review* (Switzerland), no. 8–9 (1976): 38–41, 56–57.

Rodman, Selden. *Conversations with Artists.* New York: Devin-Adair, 1957.

Rose, Barbara. *American Painting: The 20th Century.* Geneva: Skira, 1970.

Taubes, Frederic. "Egg Tempera Painting." *American Artist* (May 1957): 20–25, 69.

## ROBERT HULL FLEMING MUSEUM
## UNIVERSITY OF VERMONT

Lattie F. Coor, President

John W. Hennessey, Provost

### MUSEUM STAFF

Ildiko Heffernan, Director
Ann Porter, Acting Curator
David Penney, Interim Registrar
Merlin Acomb, Exhibition Preparator
Anna Seyller, Financial Coordinator
Mary Ann Ricketson, Community Relations
Lillian Haversat, Museum Store Manager
Patricia Brennan, Secretary